# SAHBAAR'S SECRET

## THE FIGHT FOR ACCEPTANCE

*Keep Reading!*

*Paul G. Wilson*

Look for Paul's Bookcase Books on

Facebook and the Web

# SAHBAAR'S SECRET

## THE FIGHT FOR ACCEPTANCE

BY

PAUL G. WILSON

A **Paul's Bookcase Books** Book

To my parents, Jack and Stella,
and my sisters, Jean, and
Terry, the Book Woman, for
their endless love and support.

# CONTENTS

CHAPTER ONE: SAHBAAR'S SECRET .................................................. 1

CHAPTER TWO: A NEW LIFE BEGINS .................................................. 13

CHAPTER THREE: STRANGERS IN THE JUNGLE ................................. 25

CHAPTER FOUR: FRIENDS TO THE RESCUE! ...................................... 39

CHAPTER FIVE: A BOLD PLAN .......................................................... 49

CHAPTER SIX: A NEW SURPRISE IN THE JUNGLE .............................. 61

CHAPTER SEVEN: CONFESSIONS AND DISCOVERIES ......................... 71

CHAPTER EIGHT: THE ENEMY RETURNS ........................................... 81

CHAPTER NINE: A TRAGIC TURN OF EVENTS ................................... 93

CHAPTER TEN: A DESPERATE PLAN .................................................. 105

CHAPTER ELEVEN: THE FINAL SHOWDOWN ..................................... 121

# CHAPTER ONE
## SAHBAAR'S SECRET

    The sun was shining brightly into the cave when Sahbaar's mother Sahandra woke him with a firm nudge of her nose. The sleepy tiger cub rolled over and stretched his paws out slowly. He wanted to sleep longer, but then he remembered that today was the first day his mother was going to take him outside of the cave. Sahbaar leaped up and headed for the opening, but his mother moved quickly to block the way. She wanted to prepare him for his first trip out into the world. At first the cub protested, but then he allowed his mother to perform the morning ritual.

    At last, it was time. Sahbaar was suddenly a bit frightened. He moved slowly over to the entrance, peeked out, and gasped. The world looked so big and strange! As the cub looked out at all the trees and bushes, he knew he wanted to see more. He took a few steps out and looked back at his mother. By doing this, he got his first look at the huge slab of granite that the lair was cut into, and the giant trees that towered over it. The tiny cub gasped in awe at the size of it all. Sahbaar's mouth hung open in wonder as he slowly turned around in a circle, taking everything in. The colors were all so beautiful, and there were so many shapes!

    The tiger sat and looked at his surroundings for a few moments, not sure what to inspect first. Then he went over and sniffed a flower, turned, and batted at a leaf as it bobbed on a low branch. The cub moved from one object to the next, studying each carefully. His mother smiled at the way he delighted in everything he saw. After a while, Sahbaar's mother took him for a short walk so that the cub could see even more new things. The next day, there were more short walks, and each time Sahbaar wanted to go further. Every walk was full of surprises, and the tiger cub found that along with seeing and smelling, he could climb and crawl over and pounce on so many new things.

    Then came the day when his mother told him he was ready to go to the clearing and meet some other animals. The tiger cub was nervous and excited at the same time. After preparing him, Sahandra led him down a trail twice as far as he had ever gone before. Finally, she pushed aside a leafy branch, and there they were. Sahbaar took a few steps into this huge open area, and then something inside of him told him to start running. He ran back and forth and in circles, as fast as he could, while his mother sat and watched proudly. Sahbaar had just begun circling the area for the third time when a branch in front of him suddenly moved. He stopped quickly before running straight into a lion cub his own size. The tiger cub blinked his wide eyes a few times in amazement, then scampered back to Sahandra and hid behind her, peeking out.

The lion cub just stood and stared as his mother walked up behind him. Sahbaar's mother stood and stepped aside, removing her cub's hiding place. Sahbaar was about to dart behind her again when she said in a gentle voice, "Sahbaar, don't be frightened. This is Taleka, and this is her son, Nero."

The lion cub stood his ground. "Not very brave, are you?" he said with a high-pitched growl.

"Nero!" his mother scolded. "That's not nice!"

Nero turned his head to look at her. "Well, he isn't!" He looked back at the tiger, staring intently. Sahbaar's curiosity was greater than his fear, and he cautiously crept forward and began to sniff the air. Nero did also, and after a few minutes, the two decided the other was all right. "I'm Nero," the lion cub finally said. "My mom says you live down that way." He nodded his head back towards Sahbaar's lair.

"Yes," the tiger replied slowly. "I'm Sahbaar." He seemed fascinated with the lion cub. "What are you?" he finally asked.

"I'm a lion," Nero replied, somewhat surprised. "My mom says you're a tiger."

"Yes," Sahbaar said again, more confidently. The two cubs stood looking at each other.

"Do you know how to wrestle?" Nero asked finally.

Sahbaar was confused. "No," he replied. "Is it like sniffing flowers?'

Nero threw his head back and laughed, and when Sahbaar did the same, the lion cub suddenly pounced, knocking the tiger onto his back. Sahbaar sat up, surprised but not hurt. At first he thought Nero was angry with him, but the other cub was smiling.

"Come on," Nero urged. "You try. Let's play!" With that, Sahbaar crouched down and then sprang, and the pair began rolling over and over together, laughing. After a while they stopped to rest, and Nero took his new friend over to a small pool to drink. At first, Sahbaar was hesitant, but after watching Nero, he slowly lowered his head and began to lap. "That's it. No problem," Nero encouraged. "It tastes good. It's just water."

When the lion said 'water', Sahbaar pulled his head back as if startled. At the same time, the now laughing lion took his large paw and pushed the tiger's head under the water. The lion stepped back, expecting his friend to be a bit angry at the prank, but Nero was shocked instead when Sahbaar jerked his head out of the pool and began howling as if in great pain. Sahandra was there in one leap, and when she saw her son's wet head, she immediately began to shoo him on ahead of her towards the path to their lair. As Sahbaar scampered off, still yelping, Sahandra turned to the troubled lion cub and his mother. "I'm sorry," she said quickly. "I should have told you. Sahbaar is deathly afraid of water." She hurried after him.

The next morning, Sahandra wanted to take her son back to the clearing, but Sahbaar did not want to leave the lair. "I'm sure Nero is there waiting to say he is sorry. He didn't know. If you are going to be upset with anyone, it should be me. I should have been more careful with you."

Sahbaar scratched at the ground. "I'm not mad at you. I guess I'm not mad at Nero, either. I'm mad at this whole thing about the water."

Sahandra lay down and pulled her son close to her. "I should have told you to be careful around the water, not fear it," she said. "I don't want you to be afraid to go out into the world. If I had taught you better, you might have been prepared for Nero's trick. I'm sorry."

Sahbaar looked at his mother lovingly. "It's all right, mother," he said, trying to soothe her now. "I will learn to live with this secret of mine, and I will be fine." Tears of pride came to Sahandra's eyes as she saw how mature her young cub was already.

From that point on, things were much better. Nero apologized, and the pair became even closer friends. Like Sahbaar, Nero was amazed by the world he lived in, and so when each cub was a bit older and stronger, their mothers led them on a trip that was much longer. This journey led them up a path, which twisted through and spiraled around one of the huge rock towers that were a part of the jungle they lived in. When they finally reached the top, the adults could show the cubs their jungle and beyond. To the east and north lay their jungle, stretching farther than the cubs could see. The thick treetops wove together in a dozen shades of green, interrupted here and there by small clumps of rock, rising above them in just as many shades of grey.

To the south lay more jungle, and a wide break in the trees where the Great River flowed. The cubs were mesmerized by so much swirling water as it splashed and crashed into large rocks along the edge and throughout its center. The western view was equally as unusual as, just a short distance from the tower they stood on, the jungle ended abruptly, and a wide field stretched far over to another similar jungle on the other side. The meadow stopped at the river to the south, but stretched out of sight to the north. The long grasses of the field swayed and churned as if they were some kind of green river, interrupted here and there by single or clumps of small bushes and a few small trees. "Look, mama!" Sahbaar exclaimed. "Another jungle across the field! May we go there someday?"

"No," his mother said firmly. "That jungle is not for us. The King forbids anyone to even set foot in it."

"Why?" the cub questioned. "Are there dangerous things there?"

Sahandra hesitated as if she wasn't sure how to answer. "It's just a bad place," she finally blurted. "Everything in it is bad. The King says so." The ever-curious Sahbaar wanted to ask more questions about the place, but his mother stopped him.

"If my father says it's a bad place, then it must be so," Nero said proudly. "He is a very wise King, and he knows how to protect his subjects." Sahbaar knew his friend must be right. The mothers carefully led their cubs back down the trail.

A few days later, Sahandra would not let Sahbaar go out and play. She told him that they would be going to a special place. "What special place?" the cub questioned, "and why?"

His mother smiled. "You'll see," was all she would say. Sahbaar's father, Lambera, watched proudly as the cub's mother carefully prepared her son so that he looked his best. Then the two parents took Sahbaar down yet another jungle path. The playful cub ran ahead, chasing butterflies. Soon, they were in an area new to the young tiger. Lambera then led the way. The path began to widen and narrow at will, from a trail four feet wide to a gap in the trees up to twenty feet across. Shrubs and clumps of long grass dotted the area, and Sahbaar ran in and out of them, ready to pounce on anything he might find. The three tigers walked for a long time.

Finally, they reached a clearing in the trees. Before them stood a wide rock slab eight feet off the ground. A jumble of flat rocks led up to this platform in one great mass. The rock mass was almost as wide as the path. When Sahbaar saw the rocks, he darted out ahead of his father, ready to climb this new challenge. He had only taken a few steps up onto the pile when Lambera stopped him. "Sahbaar, no!" the large tiger growled sharply. "You must not go up there!"

Confused, the cub hesitated, looking up at the flat summit for a moment before turning and coming back down. "Why can't I go up there?" the cub questioned his father.

"Because it is for the King and the Jungle Council only," his mother replied.

The cub scrunched up his face. "The Jungle Council? Who are they?"

"You'll see," his mother said with a smile. "Today is the day you learn about many new things." Sahandra began to lead Sahbaar around the Council platform. As they reached the side of the structure, Sahbaar looked around in awe and wonder at the new area before him.

The tigers had come around the left side of the rocks. The space between the rocks and the trees was only six or seven feet wide. However, as they neared the front corner of the rock structure, the tree line stopped abruptly. In its place, the ground sloped up gently to the left to a great height. It was oddly absent of any vegetation other than short grasses and an occasional clump of weeds. Sahbaar would learn soon why this was so. As Sahandra led him out further, the cub looked around to see that, across from a small flat area, the land also sloped upward, as well as to the right of this flat area. These hills and flat area were also nearly bare, except for the trees that lined the top all the way around.

The area before them was actually a small valley, with hills on three sides and a small field at the bottom in front of the rock platform. Unlike the back, the front of the platform was a straight wall, with a one-foot ridge that hung over at the top. This natural theater was quite impressive, but that was not what had caused the cub to stop short and stare in awe. It was the ever-growing stream of animals, which were beginning to fill the hillside from all sides. Nero and his mother Taleka were the only other animals Sahbaar had seen up close, and they looked much like him. A few other times when Sahbaar's mother took him on walks, he had seen strange looking creatures in the distance. Now, here they all were, and as the area began to fill up and the animals pressed together, the cub began to get worried. Some of the beasts were huge!

Sahbaar's mother nudged at him, and directed him to the right. She guided her cub to the front of the group, along the edge of the flat field while his father went up into the crowd. It was a little farther down that Sahbaar met Nero.

"Hi!" Nero called above the din, "welcome to the Gathering Place. What do you think of all this?"

Sahbaar was still looking around. "What are all these things, and why are they all here?" he finally said.

Nero giggled. "These are all the kinds of animals that live in our jungle."

"So, why are they here?" Sahbaar repeated.

Nero was surprised. "Doesn't your mother tell you anything?" he teased. "This is a New Moon Gathering. The creatures of the jungle gather here the day after each new moon. The Jungle Council and King give us information, like changes in the jungle or weather, so that we can be prepared."

"My mother says the Jungle Council stands on the rock platform," Sahbaar commented. "Who are they?"

Nero rolled his eyes. "Don't know that either? They are a group of very smart animals that the King picked to help him make decisions and rule. They are all very important and respected."

"I guess I don't know too much," Sahbaar admitted in a small voice.

"Oh, that's all right," Nero said quickly. "I just know about it because my dad is the King. All you have to do now is sit and listen to what the Council has to say. Just try and learn things as you go."

"Thanks, Nero," Sahbaar replied. "You're a true friend."

The crowd got quieter for a moment as the Council began to appear one by one on the platform. Nero whispered the name of each one in Sahbaar's ear. As each Council member came up from the center of the back, they would walk ceremoniously to the front, then to the left or the right, alternately. When they were all in place, there was one space left in the center. Together, they all stepped back until they were lined up near the back of the platform. Then, Rahshar the Great King appeared and stepped to the front center of the platform. The crowd was still talking and making noise, so the King nodded to his right, and a huge black bird perched on a stone at the right front corner of the platform began to screech loudly and flap its wings. Everyone became silent.

"Dear subjects," Rahshar roared so all could hear, "welcome to another New Moon Gathering. You are all looking very well. Maharah has the announcements for this Gathering."

As Rahshar walked to the back of the platform, a huge elephant stepped forward to take his place. The crowd had begun to murmur again, but when he cleared his throat loudly, they all became silent.

"Here are today's announcements," he began in a booming voice. "We have been informed by many animals that there are scattered areas of loose rocks along the hills to the north of the bamboo grove. Mothers, please don't let your cubs play on these rocks, as great injury might occur. As before, we will have a group of monkeys check this area, and when the rocks have finished falling and have settled, we will inform you that the area is safe. Also, the fire caused by the dark sky light flash in the large valley to the south has left many without homes. They will be moving to other parts of the jungle soon, so many of you will now have new neighbors. Welcome them.

"Speaking of weather, the Season of the Great Rains will be here soon. Mothers, be sure to teach your cubs of this, including all the dangers and warning signs. Last season, there were too many cubs that were nearly lost due to foolish behavior around flood waters. This should not happen!" He spoke these last lines with anger in his voice.

When he had finished speaking he stepped back once more, and Rahshar moved back to the front. "That concludes this New Moon Gathering. Please leave in an orderly manner, and live good lives. Remember to respect each other, and obey the laws of the jungle." With that, the Council slowly left the platform in the reverse order that they had come in. When they were gone, the animals all left leisurely, for it was forbidden to hunt during or after any ceremony or meeting at the Gathering Place.

As the animals were leaving, Sahbaar noticed all the different types of cubs that there were. Some were like him but others were very different. "Mama, can I play with some of those cubs?" he asked.

His mother smiled. "Soon, you will meet many more cubs. Just be patient."

Another morning, Sahbaar was getting ready to go out and play with Nero, but his mother stopped him. "We are going to a new place today," she told him. He asked her where, but all she said was, "you will see". Again and again he questioned her, but all she said was, "you will see. The others will be there by now."

*Others?* The cub wondered. He scampered after his mother, who had headed off in a new direction. Sahbaar followed his mother through another new area of the jungle. Finally, they stepped through some vines and into an even larger field than the one where he had met Nero. The whole area was filled with many of the different kinds of cubs that he had seen at the Gathering Place, each with a mother, or father, or both. Sahbaar looked at his mother, and she nodded.

The tiger cub walked out into the open area and looked around. He wondered if he would see his friend Nero there. Just then, the lion cub and his mother appeared. Sahbaar ran over to him. "Do you know any of these cubs?" he asked.

Nero shook his head. "No, this is my first time here." The pair looked around again and watched the other cubs as they played. A young crocodile was chasing a young, laughing bear. Sahbaar was amazed at how fast the crocodile could move, as it kept up with the hairy beast. They passed a mother rhinoceros, whose son huddled close to her. Suddenly, he joined the chase, laughing also as he lumbered along. Sahbaar smiled as the trio weaved between and around the other animals. A leopard cub jumped in front of the young bear, snarling fiercely. The bear stopped quickly, playfully raising up on its back legs and roaring back at the leopard, which bounded away, laughing.

The crocodile stopped short to avoid running into the bear, but the rhino wasn't paying attention and stepped on the crocodile's tail before stumbling off to the side. The crocodile yelped loudly, and its mother scurried up. "Ahgrah, my baby, what happened?" she cried, checking her daughter's tail.

The young rhinoceros was very upset. "I'm so sorry!" he said sadly. "I didn't mean to hurt you. I couldn't stop in time. Are you all right?" He looked like he was about to cry. The rhino's mother appeared then. "Gahdar, what did you do?" she questioned.

The crocodile's mother spoke up quickly. "It's all right. It was an accident. My daughter is fine."

"Yes, I'm O.K.," the young Ahgrah said. "I was more surprised than hurt." The two mothers sighed with relief, and then wandered off, talking.

Sahbaar watched this whole scene with great interest. He wondered if the baby crocodile was truly all right. "Let's go check it out," he said to Nero, but just then the lion's mother called to him. The tiger bounded over to the crocodile and rhino.

Gahdar was still trying to apologize. "I'm Sahbaar," the tiger said. "Are you all right?"

"Like I keep telling Gahdar, I am fine!" Ahgrah said. "You don't have to say you're sorry anymore!" she told him.

"But I just feel so bad," the baby rhino pouted.

The crocodile rolled her eyes. "Well, if you feel that bad..." With a quick whip of her tail, she slapped the rhino's side.

"Ouch!" Gahdar said in surprise.

"There!" Ahgrah said with a smile, winking. "Now we're even!" Gahdar looked confused, but when Ahgrah started laughing, the rhino did, too.

Sahbaar joined the laughter just as Nero walked up. "What's so funny?" the lion asked, grinning.

"I just made some new friends," Sahbaar remarked, introducing the crocodile and rhinoceros to the lion. Gahdar excitedly told Nero what had just happened, and Nero began to laugh also.

The four friends sat and talked for a while. Sahbaar discovered that Gahdar and Ahgrah both lived just a short distance from the tiger's lair. Nero lived a bit further away, but not too far for the friends to play together. Sahbaar knew they were all going to be good friends for a long time.

The weeks passed. The four spent at least part of each day together, running and laughing under the trees. Sahbaar and Nero took turns making up games where the animals would rescue each other from imaginary foes. The games were fun and exciting, but very simple and safe. The young friends had no way of knowing that someday these games would be very real.

Sahbaar's large paw swatted Nero's head playfully as the two cubs rolled and tumbled on the soft jungle floor. Nero swatted back, and the tiger cub rolled under a bush. Sahbaar sat up and quickly sprang at the lion, growling his fiercest growl.

The lazy air was suddenly pierced by Gahdar's voice. "Sahbaar, Nero, my horn has grown bigger!" the baby rhinoceros shouted proudly, crashing through the bushes.

"So it has," Sahbaar replied. The trio began a chase game under the swaying trees. Soon, they stopped to rest. "Say, I'm hot!" Gahdar said. "Let's go for a swim in the river!"

"Um - ah - I can't," Sahbaar stammered. "I have to collect my tasha berries."

Ahgrah had just come through some tall grass and had heard what her friends had said. "It's all right," she said gently. "Nero has told us of your fear of the water. We want to help you learn that there is nothing to be afraid of." Gahdar nodded excitedly in agreement.

"No, really," the tiger cub insisted, "I have to collect my berries. I really must!"

"You always have to collect tasha berries!" Nero growled. "Every day! We lions are hunters, just like you tigers. *I* don't have to collect any berries!"

"Well, tigers are different," came the reply. Sahbaar turned quickly as if embarrassed, and scampered off in search of the orange berries. He could never tell his friends the real reason why he couldn't go swimming with them, or why he had to climb the tasha trees and collect the berries. It was his family's secret, and he had to do his part. Once he was out of sight of the others, he trudged down the path sadly.

Nero went to the river with Gahdar and Ahgrah. He longed to follow his tiger friend, but the last time he did, his endless questions about the berry gathering had brought Sahbaar to tears. "I still think it's too bad," Nero said as he splashed around. "Sahbaar won't even let us try to help him. He also acts strangely. Why does he always have to collect those berries? I never heard of such a thing!"

"Maybe it really is just how tigers are," Ahgrah remarked. The baby crocodile slid down a rock into the water. "You are right about the fear of water, though. I know we could cure him of that."

"He can't ever go swimming," Gahdar added sadly. "And what does he do when it rains? Does he have to stay in his lair?"

"Do you think he will be like this forever?" Ahgrah asked.
"I hope not," Nero said. "I wish I could do something."

Sahbaar was not really afraid of water. Late that very night, like every night, his mother led him to the river where he splashed all alone while she kept watch over him. After all the orange tasha berry juice had washed off, a very white tiger cub with brown stripes shook himself off and led his mother home.

Sahbaar sighed as he walked along. Bathing alone at night made the cub long even more to splash and swim with his friends. His mother noticed the glum look and comforted him. "Sahbaar, your difference does not make you bad. Remember, your father and I will always love you very, very, much. But you *are* different. The other animals would not understand. You must always hide your difference."

The cub was still upset, and he walked on quietly. He followed a trail of fallen leaves, stepping from leaf to leaf without looking up. After a while, Sahbaar looked up and said, "Mama, tell me the story again."

"What story?" his mother replied, pretending not to know and trying not to smile.

"You know, the one about when I was born, and how Father figured out what to do," Sahbaar said, suddenly impatient.

His mother sighed. "Sahbaar, I tell you that story *every night*!" The cub scampered back to his mother and rubbed against her leg, purring. "Oh, all right, I'll tell you if you promise to go right to sleep." They were almost back at the lair now, and Sahbaar bounded over to the entrance and went in. By the time his mother got there, he was lying on his grass mat, eagerly waiting. She came in and lay down next to him.

"On the night you were born," she began slowly, "it was very warm and peaceful. Your father was very anxious, and he paced all around the lair. Then, you were born." She looked down at her son, and her voice became softer. "Oh, you were such a cute little thing," she cooed. "Not much bigger than my paw. We both loved you immediately."

Sahbaar smiled. "Then Papa noticed my color?" he urged her on. "Yes," she continued, "your father said to me, 'Is he supposed to be white? Where is the orange, and why are his stripes brown?' I told him I didn't know, since you were our first cub and the first I had ever seen. 'Maybe the orange grows in later', I had said, 'and the stripes turn black.' Your father left to see if he could find the answer. He met another male tiger who he knew had a young male cub. He asked this male what his son had looked like when he was born. 'Why, just like me!' the other father replied with a big grin, 'only much smaller, of course. Why do you ask?' 'Oh, no reason,' your father had said quickly. 'My mate and I are going to have a cub soon, and I was just curious.'"

"He was afraid the King would find out," Sahbaar interrupted again. "Yes, your father knew the King did not approve of any animals that looked different. The King was afraid those animals might be dangerous and do bad things."

"Were you worried?" Sahbaar asked. His mother was growing impatient with him and gave him a stern look. "Yes, we were very worried. We were afraid the King would take you away from us. We decided not to let anyone see you until we could figure out what to do. I was hoping by then that the orange fur and black stripes would grow in. After a few weeks, it didn't look like that was going to happen. Your father kept trying to think of a way to color your fur orange and black..."

"Then he found the berries!" Sahbaar nearly shouted, springing to his feet.

"Who's telling this story?" Sahandra growled. "Now, lie down and let me finish!" The cub obeyed, and his mother continued. "Your father went for a walk to think about what to do. A bird cried out, and when he looked up at it, he stepped on some tasha berries that had fallen from their tree. When he raised his paw and saw the orange juice on his white fur, he got an idea.

"He came running into the lair with a bunch of tasha berries in his mouth. When I asked what he was going to do with them, he dropped them on you and began to smoosh them into your fur. I thought he was crazy! I roared, 'What are you doing?'" She said all of this very dramatically, and the cub began to roll around with laughter.

"Then, I saw how the berries had stained your fur," she continued, calming him down. "Turning it orange, and your stripes black. I was hoping the color would stay on, but it didn't. Your father had just finished carefully coloring you to look like a regular tiger cub when you discovered your first water puddle over by the doorway, where some rain had come in the night before." Sahandra laughed. "After just a few minutes of splashing, the *puddle* was orange, and you were white and brown again!" Sahbaar tried to ask her another question, but his mother shushed him. "We decided we would just have to keep you away from water when there were others around. Your father also realized that instead of 'painting' you with the juice, he could just roll you around in it. That's when he made the pit. He made sure it was large enough for when you started to grow. Then, each morning, he would place some berries in the pit, make you lay on your side in them, and then he would roll you back and forth to teach you what to do." As she said this, Sahandra placed her front paws on Sahbaar's tummy and began to roll him back and forth. She started to tickle him, and the cub squirmed and yelped with delight.

"So that's how you learned to color your fur" Sahbaar's mother ended the story. "Now, go to sleep! There will be time for more talk tomorrow." After nuzzling noses, which is a tiger kiss, Sahbaar rolled over and fell asleep, looking at the berry pit.

## CHAPTER TWO
## A NEW LIFE BEGINS

The next morning, Sahbaar woke early. He scampered to the back of the cave to the shallow pit his father had dug. After rolling around carefully on his back in the tasha berries he had put there the day before, he was once again an orange, black, and white tiger. He finished by licking some splotches of orange off his tummy and cleaning the bottoms of his paws so they were white again. When the juice on his fur had dried, he was ready to go.

Nero was waiting at the cave entrance. "Why must you always take so long?" he questioned. Sahbaar answered with a swat, and the two were off tumbling again. Today, the adventurers were going to explore a new trail Nero had discovered near his lair. As they moved down the path, each pretended they were on the hunt and chose different small bushes or plants as 'prey' to stalk and pounce on. When they came to the top of a small hill, Sahbaar stopped to stretch up on his toes and take a deep breath of the sweet jungle air. Just then, Nero pounced on him, and the two rolled down the hill, laughing.

At the bottom of the hill, Nero rolled against a small bush next to a huge rock. He bumped his head gently against the rock, and Sahbaar began to laugh. Nero started to chase him, and the tiger leaped for the safety of another bush at the base of the rock. Nero sat back and prepared to laugh as he thought Sahbaar would bump his own head, but instead the tiger seemed to disappear into the tiny shrub! Nero quickly ran over and sniffed at the bush. "Sahbaar, where are you?" he called out.

"I'm in here!" his friend called back. "There is a cave behind the bush!"

"Really?" Nero replied. He pushed some of the greenery aside to see the tiger's face peeking out of a small hole. Nero dug out some of the dirt on the side of the hole to make it a bit bigger. He was careful not to tear away any of the bush so that the opening would remain hidden. When he was done, the lion joined Sahbaar inside.

"This is great!" the tiger roared, as his eyes adjusted to the dark and he looked around. "Our own cave!"

"Yes," Nero added, "and the bushes completely hide the opening. It can be our secret!" The pair proceeded to search every bit of the cave. It was long and narrow. About halfway back, there was a large space off to one side. The two agreed it would be the perfect place to wait and pounce on anyone who should discover and then wander into their cave.

"Look," Nero said, exploring the back end of the cave. "There's even a secret exit, in case we get trapped!" He squeezed out through a small hole in the rocks and then peeked back inside. "Come on," he urged his friend, "try it!" Sahbaar crawled through, and the pair laughed as they ran around the front to do it again. Then they went the other way, in the back and out the front, laughing the whole time.

Soon, they both collapsed on the cave floor, panting. In the still dimness, they could hear water dripping steadily from the ceiling. Sahbaar moved a bit closer to investigate. "No!" Nero cried, "It is water!"

"I'm not afraid of water, I just don't like getting it on me," the tiger reassured his friend. "I can drink it. But thank you for thinking of me."

"We all don't care about your fear-um-dislike of water," the lion said. "You are still our friend."

Sahbaar was deeply moved. "I believe you will be my best friend for life," he said solemnly.

"And you are mine!" Nero replied cheerfully. The two friends beamed at each other.

"We need to have a ceremony," Nero said. "Every great event has a ceremony!"

Sahbaar looked around. He found a piece of broken gourd and pushed it over to where the water was dripping. When the gourd was full, the tiger pushed it between himself and Nero. In his deepest, strongest voice, Sahbaar announced, "I, Sahbaar, declare Nero is my best friend for life!" He bent his head and lapped up some of the water. The tiger then nodded to Nero.

In a voice even deeper and more booming, the lion replied, "I, Nero, declare Sahbaar is my best friend for life," and then drank. Then Sahbaar roared at Nero. The lion roared back, and they both laughed.

The two pals went back outside to play. They stalked and ran together all day. That night after bathing, Sahbaar was so tired he could barely walk home. Back in the lair, he immediately fell into a deep sleep.

The white and brown tiger woke to the sound of his friend's voice calling from the lair entrance. "Come on, Sahbaar, get up. I want to go down the trail again."

Sahbaar's sleepy eyes drifted over to the berry pit. He gasped. The cub had been having so much fun the day before that he had forgotten to gather his berries! His mother was just leaving, and Sahbaar quickly asked her to find some. "I'm sorry," his mother explained, "but I have to go out and hunt. You should have remembered to gather them. That is your part of the secret. Now you must stay in the lair. Do not go out, or let anyone in. You can get more berries tonight after dark." The adult tiger bounded off in search of food.

"I can't come out today," the tiger cub called to the waiting Nero. "I don't feel well."

"Then we can play here," Nero called back. "Let's wrestle."

"No-no," the tiger's voice echoed back quickly. "Please. I must be alone."

Nero turned slowly and trudged off, confused. Inside the cave, Sahbaar cried, wishing he was not different

Nero, Gahdar, and Ahgrah wondered more about Sahbaar. There had to be a reason for the strange way he acted. Perhaps Cheerah would know something. The four friends had met her one day when they were playing under some fruit trees. Gahdar had just been commenting how hungry he was, when suddenly fruit started dropping out of the tree, landing right at his feet! As Sahbaar, Nero, Ahgrah, and Gahdar all stared with open mouths, there came a wave of screeching laughter. Then, a large gibbon dropped out of the tree and said to the rhino, "Is that enough?" Everyone burst out laughing, and Cheerah introduced herself. From then on, she played often with the others. It was Cheerah who first tied vines together to create a ball for the others to run with and kick to each other. She would join in, and this became one of the group's favorite games.

Because she was older, Cheerah knew many things about the jungle, and she was happy to teach the others. She had also been to the Man lair, and told her friends about these strange creatures. The 'lair' was an animal hospital, and the doctors there had found her orphaned in another jungle. They had raised her until she was old enough to be on her own, and then brought her to this jungle. She had learned many more things from them, and she promised to go and try to learn about Sahbaar's strange behavior from Man.

One day, Sahbaar and Nero followed another trail farther from home than they had ever gone. As they tumbled around in a field, the clouds darkened and it began to rain softly. Sahbaar jumped up and turned to run. "Wait!" Nero shouted, "There are no light flashes or sky roars, and the water will not hurt you. It is safe!"

"No!" Sahbaar cried. "I must go quickly!"

Nero leaped onto his friend and held him down. "Sahbaar, please! It will be all right. The water is nothing to fear!"

The tiger cub squirmed. "No, no, please!" He wriggled free and scampered off. Nero gasped. The back legs of his fleeing friend were *white*! Nero was shocked. Suddenly, his good friend looked so different, not like his friend at all. Nero wanted to run after the tiger, but he was afraid. Slowly, he turned and walked back to his lair, more confused than ever.

Back in his own lair, Sahbaar looked himself over. The orange berry juice had washed off much of his legs and back in large patches. He was sure Nero had seen, and he wondered what his friend was thinking. Sahbaar sat down and began to cry again.

Nero sat in his lair, not sure what to think. He couldn't believe what he had seen. Perhaps he hadn't seen it at all. There were a lot of open holes in the treetops there on the path. Maybe he had just seen bright sunlight shining on Sahbaar's back and legs. Nero hoped that was what he had really seen.

The next morning, Sahbaar took longer than usual to roll in the berry pit. It was piled extra high with berries, which the cub had gathered the night before after bathing. "Why do you have so many berries?" his mother asked, "and why are you rolling around so hard? You might hurt yourself!"

"I don't care!" the cub growled, thrashing around. "I want the color to go on and never come off. I want to be a normal tiger!"

Sahbaar's mother sat him down. "Let me tell you a story. It's a story about your uncle."

Sahbaar frowned in confusion. "What uncle, mama?" he asked.

"His name was Bahar, and he was my brother," she replied. "When he was a young tiger out on a hunt here, he fell off some rocks and broke his leg. It didn't heal right, and he could never run well after that. Still, he had to try."

"Did his leg ever get better?" the cub questioned.

"No," Sahandra said. "It never did. He just had to learn to live with his difference. You must also learn to live with your difference"

"Where is Uncle Bahar now?" Sahbaar asked.

Sahandra shook her head sadly. "I don't know. My parents told me he just went off to another jungle one day." Sahbaar could see this made his mother sad, so he said no more about it.

The lion and tiger cubs continued to play together every day. Nero stopped asking questions about the tiger. Luckily, Gahdar and Ahgrah lost interest in Sahbaar's strange habits, also. Everyone accepted the unusual behavior of their friend. Things were fine until that one morning.

Sahbaar and Nero had been hunting all day, and the tiger had forgotten to gather the berries again. The next morning, the white and brown tiger slipped out of the lair, hoping he could find some quickly. Unfortunately, Gahdar was coming down the path, and he bellowed in fear as he saw this unusual sight. Sahbaar ran up the path and leaped back into the lair. The baby rhinoceros ran around, telling everyone he saw that he had seen a terrible white and brown beast with huge fangs and claws run into the tiger lair. Sahbaar's mother had just returned, and knew the rhino was talking about her son. She ducked into the lair for a moment and saw her frightened son cowering in the corner. Sahandra went back out and declared loudly that the cave was empty.

As Nero approached, he overheard all the animals talking excitedly. Listening to their remarks, he suddenly realized the connection between this monster Gahdar had described, the orange berries, and the white patches he thought he saw on his friend's back and legs. The lion immediately knew what he had to do. He found a tasha tree and leaped against the trunk, shaking the branches until bunches of the berries rained down on him. He quickly snatched as many berry bunches as he could, ran back to the lair and, sneaking around the ever-growing crowd, slipped inside.

When Sahbaar saw his friend, he shrank in fear. "What are you doing here?" he yelped. "You shouldn't be here!" The tiger cub tried to burrow even deeper into the corner.

"It's all right," Nero said calmly. "I know what is going on. I figured it out."

Sahbaar looked surprised for a moment, and then burst into tears. "What am I going to do?" he wailed. "I'm trapped in here!"

"Not when we have these!" Nero replied, nudging the berries at his feet with his paw.

Sahbaar finally noticed the berries. "Oh, Nero, thank you so much! Here, spread them out in the pit so that I can roll around in them."

"No time," Nero said. "That crowd will be pushing in here at any moment. We have to fix you fast so that you can go out and face them." The lion cub picked up a bunch of berries with his teeth, and holding them against his friend's side, mushed them with his paw.

"We're not going to have enough," Sahbaar wailed.

"Be quiet, and start squashing berries!" Nero growled. The pair did their best to cover as much of the tiger's body as they could. They could hear animals demanding to enter the lair, and Sahandra pleading with them to leave her family alone.

The crowd of animals grew loud. They pushed their way forward, trying to get inside. Just then, Sahbaar and Nero walked out. Everyone stared. Though Nero had tried to help, he had not done a very good job. The young tiger was a mixture of black and brown stripes and orange and white splotches! His friend's paws were stained with the berry juice. A curious elephant, braver than the others, stepped forward and touched a wet orange spot on the tiger and examined the end of his trunk carefully. Then, he sucked up some water from a nearby puddle and sprayed the cub. The entire group of animals gasped at the now white and brown tiger.

The crowd began to grumble. What was to be done with this different one? There was such a fuss that no one noticed the arrival of Cheerah. The gibbon moved through the treetops until she was at the front of the crowd. There, she saw Sahbaar's mother trying to defend her son and the lion Nero. When Cheerah saw the white and brown cub, her eyes grew wide. The gibbon sat above the crowd and listened as the older animals mumbled to each other as they stared at the strange creature. Someone had gone to tell Rahshar, and when he arrived, he quieted the crowd with a loud roar. Nero watched hopefully as his father, the King of beasts, prepared to speak. He hoped Rahshar would make things right. The lion cub held his breath and waited.

"This is indeed a serious thing," the King began slowly. "His difference may not have changed him yet, but we do not know how he will be when he is older. Perhaps bad things will happen." The older animals all nodded and mumbled their agreement. Rahshar looked into his son's eyes and hesitated. "A decision this important must not be rushed into. I will have to discuss this with the Jungle Council." Since all the members were present, they huddled together, oddly enough, under a huge tasha tree.

As they decided Sahbaar fate, Nero stood close by the tiger. "No matter what happens, I will still always be your friend."

Sahbaar smiled back at him. "I will be yours, also." Forgetting for a moment the trouble Sahbaar was in, the pair began wrestling and laughing. Many in the crowd frowned and muttered their disapproval. They felt the two should not be playing during such a serious time.

The Council meeting went on for a while. The other animals stood waiting by the tiger lair, eager to hear the decision. They could hear several Council members arguing, though they could not make out the words. Then there was silence. The Council trudged back to the group at the lair, with Rahshar in the lead. There was a very solemn look on his face. "We are all in agreement," he said firmly. "There is no choice but to banish this different one from our jungle." All the animals gasped again.

"No...No!" cried Sahbaar's mother desperately. The Council decision was now law, and could not be changed.

"The cub has not fully learned how to hunt yet!" Sahbaar's father argued. "Surely he will have a very difficult time!"

Rahshar thought a moment but then replied, "He is a clever cub. He will learn on his own." The King knew he had hurt his son also, but he had to be firm. "Sahbaar, I will let you say your farewells, but then you must leave. I am sorry, but it is the law!"

Sahandra's sorrow turned to anger. "If my child is to be banished, then I shall be banished also!"

The King did not hesitate for a moment. "I'm sorry," he said to the mother tiger, "but I cannot allow it. Sahbaar might hurt you someday if you went with him, and if I were to learn that even one of my subjects came to harm because of something I allowed, I could not live with it."

Sahbaar tried to be strong as he hugged his parents. His mother cried and cried. "Oh, my precious son, how I wish your father and I could go with you! We will love you always, and will think of you every day."

Sahbaar hugged Nero also, who whispered in his ear, "I'm sorry."

"It is all right. I will be fine, and someday I will come back," the tiger said bravely.

"These guards will escort you to the border," Rahshar said. As he spoke, two large bears appeared, one on either side of the cub.

"Let's go," one said gruffly. Sahbaar looked back at his parents, then turned, and head held high, began to march off with the guards.

It took all day for Sahbaar to walk to the edge of the jungle. It was farther from his home than he had ever been. He thought about running off and hiding in the brush, then sneaking back to his lair, but the bears would surely find him. Hearing a noise, the cub looked up and saw birds circling above him. For a minute, he wished he was a bird. He would be free to be himself, because if someone did not like his difference, he would just fly away. While he was watching the birds, he also saw dark clouds moving in swiftly. Soon the rains came, and still the birds seemed to follow him, keeping watch. Sahbaar had a feeling someone would always be watching.

The tiger cub walked for a while in the rain. Since he had always hidden from the wet weather, it was a strange new experience for him, and he liked the feeling. By the time he reached the field that separated the two jungles, it was early in the evening. The rain began to come down harder. The winds also began to blow, and the cub quickly became very cold. The bears stopped him at the field's edge. "This is as far as we go," the first said. "You must cross the field to the other jungle, which is your new home. You must stay there and never return."

"If you should try to return, the border birds will see you," the other bear continued, pointing up to the treetops. The birds that had been following Sahbaar were now sitting on the branches, and when the cub looked up at them, they all began to flap their wings and caw loudly. "Don't be fooled by their small number," the second guard continued. "Though there are only a few of them, there are more than enough to patrol the entire border, and they can see the very smallest detail from far away, and can fly very fast."

"The border birds report directly to the King," the first guard added, "and they are very good at their job. Don't test them. Now go, you freak!" The bear pushed Sahbaar forward. The words hurt as much as the shove. The tiger cub trudged sadly out into the field, head down. The rain began to beat at the cub, so soon he was scampering towards his new home. He stopped inside the tree line of the new jungle and took one last look back. The bears were gone, but the birds were still there.

Because the wind whipped the rain back and forth, the trees of the new jungle did not shelter him. The cub searched for a cave. At last, when he thought he could walk no farther, he saw an opening in the base of a tall rock tower. Sahbaar dragged himself inside and collapsed on a tuft of grass, exhausted.

As tired as he was, the cub could not sleep. The new cave felt so strange. He laid very still, thinking of his parents and trying not to cry. Then he heard a noise. Something was in the cave with him! Sahbaar began to imagine all kinds of huge beasts lurking in the darkness, and he scampered back to the cave entrance. He sat at the entrance, not sure what to do. Then he realized he would have to start trying to be brave if he were going to survive in the new jungle. He was going to have to take care of himself. Thinking back to what his father had taught him, he decided to confront this stranger. Standing just outside of the cave so he could run off if he had to, he stood tall and looked into the darkness. The tiger growled. "Whoever is in the cave," he said loudly, "I am Sahbaar the Mighty Tiger. I am new to this jungle, and I am now claiming this cave for my lair. If you do not wish to deal with me, then you had better leave now!" He stepped to the side and waited.

Much to his relief, only a few small mice scampered out of the darkness. Sahbaar sighed and went back to his bed. After he made himself comfortable, he lay very still listening to the sounds of the new jungle. Suddenly, he gasped as he heard the sound of heavy breathing inside the cave very near to him! His heart began to race when he realized something had not been frightened by his command and was brave enough to stay in the cave. Sahbaar was quite frightened, but the breathing was calm and steady, and did not sound threatening. The white tiger decided he could share his new home with whoever was already living here. At last the cub slept, and slept deeply.

The late morning sun warming the tiger finally woke him. He blinked and squinted in the bright light, breathing deeply. The air was fresh and sweet, and Sahbaar realized he was very hungry. He slowly looked around his new home and smiled, but when his eyes drifted to the far corner, he scrambled to his feet and jumped back. There, staring down at him from a ledge just a few feet off the ground, was a large tiger! At once, the cub tried to hide his fear as he stared at the stranger. The other tiger in turn looked at Sahbaar with a mixture of surprise and relief. "Are you a white tiger?" he said in amazement.

"Yes, I am!" Sahbaar snapped, "So say what you will!"
"Oh, no, I mean no insult," the other replied gently. "I am just a very old beast, and seeing you now after your speech last night, I was afraid you were a spirit here to take me to the next life. I am certainly not ready for that! I am very happy to find instead that you are only a very unusual cub."

Sahbaar was embarrassed. "Please forgive my anger. I have hidden my difference since I was born, and now that I no longer do so, others have been very cruel."

"I am not surprised," the other replied.
Sahbaar smiled. "My name is Sahbaar, and I come from the jungle to the east."

The adult tiger's eyes opened wider when he heard these words. "I, too, once lived in the jungle to the east. My name is Bahar."

Sahbaar couldn't believe his ears. "My mother told me of an uncle I never met named Bahar. Her name is Sahandra." Now the other was greatly surprised.

"Sahandra is my sister! I have not seen her for the longest time. Is she well?" Sahbaar nodded. "Now she has a fine son, and I have a nephew!" Sahbaar smiled. The old tiger then looked around. "Where is she?" Bahar asked.

Sahbaar grew sad suddenly. "Back in the old jungle," he replied. "She left you out here alone?! That does not sound like my sister!"

"She had no choice," Sahbaar answered him, "because I was banished."

Bahar shook his head slowly. "Because you are a white tiger, no doubt, and you are a danger to the rest of the jungle."

Sahbaar couldn't believe the old tiger was speaking Rahshar's very words. "How do you know this?" he asked.

"Because, long ago, I too was banished," the old one replied.

Now Sahbaar was confused. "Banished? My mother told me that after you broke your leg and it did not heal right, you could not keep up with the others, so one day you just left."

Bahar began to laugh, and that made him cough violently. It was then Sahbaar first noticed how weak and sickly his uncle was. The cub scampered over to a small rainwater pool, which flowed into the cave from under the rock wall. Grabbing a large piece of a broken gourd with his teeth, he dipped it into the water. Sahbaar then dragged it up to his uncle, who lapped it up gratefully. Bahar thanked his nephew and continued. "No doubt that was the story your grandparents told your mother. They did not want her to know the truth - that a young Rahshar, new King of the jungle, banished me because of this." He moved one of his back legs to uncover the other, which was much shorter and thinner. "I was born with my leg this way, and my parents hoped it would grow, but it did not. Still, I had friends and was no danger to anyone. But Rahshar saw any flaw as a danger. I heard he once banished a parrot for having a crooked beak!"

Sahbaar was surprised, but he felt better. At least he wasn't the only different one. He couldn't believe how unfair Rahshar was. Bahar agreed with this and comforted his nephew. "Don't let it trouble you," he said. "What is done is done, and we must move on." All this talking had made Bahar's throat dry again, and he began to cough more violently.

As he lapped up the rest of the water in the gourd, Sahbaar could see just how old and thin he looked. Bahar's fur hung from his bones, and he wheezed as he drank. "Uncle Bahar, how long has it been since you have been out of this cave?" the tiger cub asked.

The elder thought for a moment. "It has been a long time," he finally replied.

"How do you survive?" the cub asked, wide-eyed. "What do you hunt?"

Bahar let out a long sigh. "Hunting was never easy for me, and it has become more difficult with age. When I first came to the jungle, I was still able to catch young or old prey as I always had. But as I grew older, the prey became too fast. When I found this cave, there were many kinds of small animals living here. For a while, I could catch them by hiding on the rock ledges and leaping on them, or more often by cornering them. After a while, though, the smaller animals stopped coming into the cave. Soon, all that was left were the mice. I fed on them awhile, but even they are becoming more clever and agile than I. Perhaps it is a sign that my time left here is almost over."

"Don't be silly," Sahbaar replied. "You have a long life ahead of you. I will hunt for you. You can teach me."

Bahar looked surprised again as he shook his head. "To banish a cub who had not even learned how to hunt yet! Rahshar has become truly cruel!"

Sahbaar shrugged his shoulders. "As you say, what is done is done. We have each other now, and Rahshar can't take that away." Bahar beamed with pride at his nephew's maturity.

So the hunting lessons began. The quick and agile cub would pounce on the mice and bring them to his uncle. As they ate, Bahar would talk to Sahbaar, giving him tips on how to stalk and trap the small creatures. Soon, Sahbaar was venturing out of the cave to practice on larger animals like rabbits. Bahar grew stronger every day, and soon he was able to walk out into the sunshine, something he hadn't been able to do in months. It felt good on his face and back, and he decided to go for a walk through the jungle with Sahbaar.

Now and then, they would see larger prey like young gazelle or zebra in the distance. As soon as these animals saw the strange white and brown creature, they ran off immediately. Bahar laughed loudly. "I can see you will have to rely on hiding in the tall grass, or behind rocks and trees more than other tigers do." Sahbaar knew that this was true, and so he laughed also. It was the first time he had ever laughed about his difference rather than be sad about it.

The unique white and brown coloring did come in handy sometimes. One day the two tigers were out walking, and they happened upon a group of hyenas finishing the remains of a large kill. Normally, a group this size would not be chased off by an old tiger and a cub, but Sahbaar decided to try something. He charged the group and leaped at them, roaring fiercely. Since they had never seen a white and brown tiger, they didn't know what to make of it and scampered off like the true cowards they were. "Very well done," Bahar commented. "You are very clever, indeed." Sahbaar felt very proud as the pair began to eat the biggest meal either had ever had.

As they lay in the soft grass digesting their meal, Sahbaar rolled over on his back and looked up at the fluffy clouds. "Uncle, why is Rahshar so unfair?"

"Now Sahbaar, we have talked about this before. Some animals are frightened by anything that is different because they don't understand it. I have heard tell that Rahshar's father was the same way. Perhaps the son learned it from him. I also think Rahshar truly believes he is protecting the others by acting as he does."

"He says I could become dangerous to the other animals because he thinks I will act differently. That's not fair! You can't know which a monkey will eat first, a mango or a fig, until he eats one!"

Bahar laughed. "It is a bit more complicated than that. Yes, it is unfair, but he is the King, and there is also the Council, and you know they will most likely agree with him."

Sahbaar rolled onto his stomach. "Don't you miss your sister? I know I miss her, and my father."

"There is nothing I would like better than to see her again," Bahar sighed. "Perhaps someday..."

# CHAPTER THREE
## STRANGERS IN THE JUNGLE

The months passed, and Sahbaar grew. He continued to hunt for himself and his uncle, who could hobble along rather quickly, but not fast enough to chase down prey. One day, the two were out hunting, and they heard a loud sound. It was the same kind of roar the sky made just before the rains came, but the sun was out and the clouds were white and fluffy. Uncle and nephew stopped and listened. The roar came again, but three times, and much more quickly than the sky could make it. The roar didn't even come from the sky; it came from a thick patch of trees to the south. Sahbaar was eager to explore, and Bahar reluctantly agreed.

The pair bounded to the edge of the trees and then began to creep in softly. They followed the sound of noises through the thick underbrush until they reached a small clearing. Peering out from under a bush, Sahbaar couldn't believe his eyes. Three strange creatures stood before them. "What are they, Uncle?" Sahbaar whispered.

"I have never seen such animals before," came the reply. "Not here, or in the old jungle. From what I have heard from others, though, they must be Man."

"So, this is Man," Sahbaar commented. "My friend Cheerah the gibbon has told me of them, but I have never seen any before."

Sahbaar was fascinated. He noticed they moved very much like Cheerah, though their fur was very loose and odd-looking. Each one was also a different size and shape. They were each holding some kind of stick, though Sahbaar had never seen a tree with branches like those. They seemed to be communicating with each other, and they also seemed to be looking for something.

Then the two tigers heard a rustling off to the left. A moment later, the men heard it too, and became silent. Beneath a tree a short distance away, a male and female antelope had stopped. One man slowly picked his stick up, held it flat, and raised it to look down its length. Suddenly, the stick made the sky noise, and the man jumped a bit. At the same time, the female antelope dropped to the ground. The male bent and nudged her with his nose, and then, not knowing what else to do, turned and charged at the man in sheer fury. The stick made another roar, and the male stopped and fell instantly.

Neither tiger could believe what they had just seen. Sahbaar had to know if the animals were all right. Without fear, he leaped out of the bushes and charged the men, roaring ferociously. This took the stunned Bahar by surprise, but the elder joined his nephew and leaped from his hiding place. Luckily, the men were taken by surprise as well, and were unable to shoot. They turned and ran into the jungle, screaming like monkeys. Rather than chase them, Sahbaar went over to the antelopes and sniffed them. He could not believe they were dead. Bahar was equally shocked and distressed. "Rahshar thinks our differences could be dangerous!" he mumbled.

The pair looked around the area and found a wolf and a water buffalo, laying together, both dead. They had the same kind of wound the antelope had. "Such a kill!" Sahbaar commented. "Can these beasts really eat so much?"

Bahar was distressed. "I don't think so. Something tells me these are wasteful creatures." The tigers both knew the food should not be wasted, but they could not bring themselves to touch one bite. Somehow, it didn't seem right. They both sat for a long time, trying to make sense of it all. Soon, the hyenas they had chased off the other day came around, and they had no problem claiming the kill.

"Man has done this," Sahbaar tried to explain. "They kill much more than they need."

"It does not matter to us," one replied. "Their waste is our feast!" He quickly joined his brothers. The two tigers turned and walked slowly back to their cave, both still very upset. Neither one saw Man again for a long while after that. They occasionally heard Man's sky roar, but it was far off, and moving away from them. Neither cat wished to go investigate. Each Man roar made them think of more wasteful killing, and this continued to upset Sahbaar the most.

The two tigers were out for a walk one day when a small, brightly colored bird landed on a tree branch just ahead of them. Sahbaar looked up briefly. It was odd, for even the animals that were familiar with the white tiger were still startled by his presence. In contrast, this stranger seemed interested and not frightened at all. Still, Sahbaar did not pay much attention to the creature. As the cats strolled on, the bird suddenly flew up on ahead, and once again landed on a branch above the large beasts. This continued for a while, with the bird working to stay ahead of Sahbaar and Bahar. Eventually, Sahbaar noticed this. He stopped abruptly, sat down in the middle of the path, and began to glare at the bird.

Bahar stopped also, trying to figure out what was going on. "Why are you following us?" Sahbaar growled. "What do you want?"

"Oh, pardon me, sir," the bird replied, mesmerized, "but I have never seen a tiger that looks like you do. You are almost as unusual as Man."

"Man!" Sahbaar snapped. "What do you know of Man?!"

"Oh, I have seen many, and followed some around. They are truly strange."

"What do you know of their sticks which make the sky roar?" Bahar broke in. "Did you know they could kill animals just by pointing these sticks at them?"

"Yes," the bird answered. "I have seen this all too often. The sticks come from no trees in these or any other jungle. They bring them from some other place."

"Where do these Man come from?" Bahar continued.

"That I do not know. Somewhere far away, I am sure."

"You seem to know an awful lot about Man," Sahbaar growled. "Are you their friend?"

The bird cackled with laughter. "Hardly!" she squawked. "Man has tried to hunt me also, but I am too quick for them!"

"So you do not share in their kill?" the white and brown one questioned.

"No – no," came the reply. "I do not eat meat like the falcon or vulture. My feast is the sweet fruits and dates of the trees - when I can get them. The other birds can be quite greedy."

Sahbaar's voice softened as he realized the bird could become an ally. "Stay with us, then, and warn us when Man is coming, and I will make sure you can get to the sweetest fruits and dates in the jungle!"

"Agreed!" the bird cackled enthusiastically.

"We are Bahar and Sahbaar," the old tiger said.

"I am Akoorah, and I will be your guard," the bird answered. So Akoorah made a nest just outside the tiger cave. As promised, Sahbaar made sure Akoorah had her own supply of fruits and nuts by chasing the other birds away from trees near the lair. The trio became very good friends.

Having a new friend like Akoorah made the white tiger think more about his old friends. It had been months since Sahbaar had seen Nero and the others, but it seemed like years. He longed to chase Gahdar down the path, leap over Ahgrah, or wrestle with Nero. Sahbaar wondered how they were, and what they were doing. Since it was a hot day, they were probably all down at the river. Though he had never been there with them, he could picture them all splashing around, laughing and shouting. Sahbaar suddenly realized he could have joined them, now that his secret was exposed. This made the idea of his banishment even harder to bear. The young tiger sighed loudly as he wondered if his old friends ever thought about him anymore.

Nero and the others had been thinking about their old friend, but not lately. For several days, they had been hearing a strange noise far away. To them, it sounded like the sky roar that came before the rain, though the sun was shining and no rain came. Gahdar seemed the most confused by this thing, and would continue to look up whenever the sound was made. Finally, being both a hunter and very curious, Nero decided to find the noise and what caused it. When he announced his plans, Gahdar and Ahgrah reluctantly agreed to join him. They would begin the next day.

Early in the morning, the trio met at the edge of Sahbaar and Nero's old trail. Even before they got there, they had heard the roars. As the three stood together, Nero waited for the roar, and when he heard it bounded off in that direction. "Hurry!" he called to the others. "We don't know how often we will hear the sound and must take advantage of each time to guide us." The others followed quickly.

Luckily, or perhaps not, the sound came often. It wasn't long before Nero felt they were almost upon it. As if it knew they were getting closer, the roar stopped coming. Following Nero's cue, the young rhino and crocodile began to search the underbrush with him, as quietly as a rhino and crocodile could. After a short while, Nero whispered, "Over here!" The two went to where the lion was and peeked out through the bushes with him.

The three hunters had stopped for a rest by their large Land Rover. They had walked through the surrounding area that morning, leaving the animals they had shot where they lie. Now they would drive back over their course and pick up their prizes. Like Sahbaar and Bahar had been, the three young animals were fascinated with these creatures and nearly walked right over to where they sat. The truck was just as interesting, and as the trio studied the scene, Cheerah happened to come up behind them. "What are you all looking at?" she said suddenly, causing Gahdar to jump.

"Strange creatures," Nero whispered back. "A new type of animal we have never seen before."

When Cheerah looked through the bushes she began to laugh, and the others had to quiet her. "That is only Man," she explained. "I have been to Man's lair many times."

"Yes, we know. You tell us all the time," Ahgrah said, rolling her eyes.

The gibbon made a face at her and then continued. "They are all very friendly, and they help animals who are sick. I have never seen these ones, though. They must have come from somewhere else."

Just then, one of the men, the short large one, pulled a rifle out of the truck. He pointed it up into the treetops as if ready to shoot and began to move it around back and forth. Then he fired a shot just for fun. The sound shocked the lion, rhino, and crocodile, who all crouched down in the grass in fright. Poor Cheerah, who had been sitting on a tall rock, was so startled that she fell off. None of them could believe this strange thin stick could make such a violent sound.

The leader of the hunters was angered. "Knock it off!" he shouted, hitting the large man in the shoulder. "Stop wasting ammo!"

"Yeah," the other remarked, stroking his beard. "What's wrong with you? You're gun crazy!"

"Shut up!" the man with the gun replied. "At least I'm not seeing things!"

The bearded man got angry. "I'm telling you guys, one of those tigers that chased us off the other day was white and brown. A white tiger with brown stripes! Do you know how much money we could get for a white tiger skin? Especially one with brown stripes?"

"Of course I do, you idiot!" came the large man's reply. "Except it wasn't a white tiger you saw. It was the white belly of the thing when it almost landed on top of us. You were just too scared to see that!'

"Was not!"

"Was too! It was a plain old tiger, with a big white belly!"

"Was not! A tiger's belly doesn't have brown stripes on it!"

"Was too a regular tiger! You're just blind!"

"Was not a regular tiger! I see better than you do!"

Finally, the leader had had enough. "All right, you two, knock it off!" he shouted, spinning around. "What are you, five years old?"

"Boss," the bearded hunter began in a convincing voice, "I swear it was a white tiger with brown stripes. Let's go back and look for it, and we'll all be rich. You'll see!"

"Well," the boss said, looking at his map thoughtfully, "I guess between our hunting and this idiot's itchy trigger finger, we've probably pretty much scared off all the animals in this area. Let's circle around with the truck and pick up our loot, and by that time, the animals in the other area will probably be all settled down. If there is a white tiger with brown stripes over there, he shouldn't be too hard to spot."

The bearded man scrambled into the truck, but the other one seemed to think for a moment as if it was his decision. When the boss finally glared at him, he put his gun in the back and climbed in.

Nero and the others thought the men were just climbing into some kind of strange little lair, and so they were quite surprised when the 'lair' began to growl and roar, and then run off! Nero froze for a moment, and then leaped out of the bushes after the vehicle. Gahdar and Ahgrah started after him, but Cheerah decided to stay behind. She was still too shaken by what she had seen. It wasn't long before Ahgrah had to stop. The young crocodile was just no good at crawling that quickly through the thick underbrush. Gahdar managed to keep up, but soon he became tired and stopped also. Nero was determined not to let the creatures get away, though. There were just too many interesting things about them, and the young lion had to learn more. How did their sticks make the sky roar, and why were these creatures in the jungle at all? Nero had to know.

It wasn't long before the truck stopped next to two young antelopes. Both the animals were just lying there, as if asleep. They certainly didn't look like they had been killed by another animal. The lion watched as Man claimed the kill for themselves. Nero was both surprised and disturbed that the men took only the heads for their horns, leaving all the meat behind. The lion continued to follow the vehicle, which moved much slower now as these hunters had to search for their kills. At each stop, the lion grew more and more confused and upset as Man took skins or heads, or even just the claws, packing them in a large box on the vehicles' roof, but left the precious meat behind. Finally, he could take no more, and he crept off quietly to find his friends.

The gibbon, rhino, and crocodile were amazed by the stories their friend told them. Cheerah was deeply upset by the things Nero said. She thought of Man as her friend, and had never seen or heard of any of them doing such things. All the Man creatures she knew were so gentle and loving. Nero said he did not know any other Man, and did not wish to meet any. What he did not tell the others was, while the actions of these beasts troubled him, he was still very curious about the strange sticks they had. He lay awake that night, wondering how the objects were able to bring the rain sound down from the skies. The lion just had to see the strange devices one more time. He decided he would track down the hunters and their moving lair the very next day.

The sun had not yet come up before Nero was out on the trail. He didn't know where the men had gone after he left them, so searching for them in the huge area could be hard. Luckily, it was not long before the young lion heard the sky roar once again. The noise came at steady intervals, so the lion was able to track it down. Unfortunately, by the time the lion got to the hunters they had stopped shooting, so he was not able to see the gun in action again. The men were all gathered around their moving lair once more, just looking around. Then they began to communicate.

"For the last time, enough with the gun, stupid!" the leader said angrily. This time, it was the bearded man who held the weapon, and he gently set it back inside the vehicle. "We're supposed to be looking for that white tiger. How are we going to find anything if you keep scaring everything away?!"

"Aw, we're not anywhere near where that white tiger jumped us," the bearded man complained. "He was all the way over in that other patch of jungle. Besides, I'm bored!"

"Humph!" the large man said. "When I shoot, I'm gun crazy, but it's all right for you to shoot because you're bored!"

"Oh, shut up!" the bearded man said, shoving the other. The large man shoved him back, and the two began to fight.

"Knock it off, you stooges!" the leader shouted. "Let's move!" While they had been talking, Nero noticed one of the strange sticks was leaning against a rock. If he could get it, he could take it back to his lair and try to figure out how the sound came out of it. The lion was going to leap out and grab it when the men started getting into the vehicle. Nero decided to wait until they left, but then the leader made some loud noises and pointed. "Go and get your rifle, stupid!" he was saying to the large man. "Do I have to watch you two every minute?" The large man got the gun, and the leader almost drove off without him. He had to run and leap into the side door, where the bearded man pulled him in.

Nero decided not to follow too closely. Luckily, the vehicle was moving slowly over the rough terrain, so it was not hard to keep up and yet stay hidden. At one point, though, the moving lair decided to speed up just as Nero was having a hard time making his way through a tangle of vines. Man was getting away! The lair disappeared as the lion continued to struggle. Breaking free of the vines, Nero listened for the lair growl. He quickly followed the sounds, and it was not long before he was very close again. As he made his way up a small hill, he could hear the growl of the moving lair getting softer again. Peeking through some bushes at the top of the hill, he saw the three hunters and their lair halfway across a large field.

The field seemed familiar. It was the same field the cat's mothers had shown them long ago. Nero realized it was also the field that separated it from the 'banishment' jungle, and was the same field the lion's best friend Sahbaar must have bravely marched through following his banishment.

Nero looked around. He wanted to get closer, but he was afraid the border birds would see him. The lion could see the border birds sitting in the trees along the boundary. Since everyone was forbidden to ever see or speak to Sahbaar again for life, Nero knew if he crossed the field the birds would think he was going to see the white tiger and would tell Rahshar. Just then, several birds took off and began circling the area. It was as if they knew Nero was there and had read his mind.

The lion didn't know what to do. He wasn't even sure what the penalty was for traveling to where someone had been banished, but he knew it must be severe. Was it worth it to try and see Man's stick, and perhaps see his old friend? After thinking awhile, he decided the hunters would come back sooner or later, and he would try for the stick another day. He watched for a few more minutes to see if they would come back right away.

The Land Rover was almost across the field by now. From the hilltop, Nero could see a long way. Just beyond the bunch of trees that lined the banishment jungle rose a large group of rock pillars. It was at the base of these rocks that Sahbaar and Bahar had their cave. As he did most mornings, Sahbaar had risen early to climb up to the top of the pillar to greet the morning sun and breathe in the fresh air. As he came around the field side of the rocks, he paused for a moment to sniff some wildflowers.

Far across the field, Nero saw something move on the rocks. At first he thought it was a fox, but it was much too large, even to be an adult male. The lion blinked hard and looked again. Could it be? Yes, it had to be his old friend Sahbaar! He would have liked to roar out a greeting, but the border birds were still circling. Nero could not believe how large his friend had grown. If it wasn't for his color, the lion would not even have recognized him. *Of course*, he thought, *I have grown too*. The lion was much larger, and his mane was even half grown in. He decided to take a chance and stick his head out of the bushes. He was hoping that the birds would not see him, but his friend somehow would.

Back across the field, the white tiger heard the sound of the Land Rover. He stared intently at this strange creature, trying to figure out what it was. It was large like a hippo, but the shape was much straighter. Sahbaar thought he could see something inside this beast. He strained to see what was moving there. The tiger was staring so intently that he did not realize the hunters had now spotted him.

"There!" the bearded man cried, pointing. "Up there! It's a white and brown tiger! I told you I saw one! I knew I did! There it is!" The large man didn't say a thing.

"Well, I'll be!" was all the leader could say. He turned the wheel sharply, and the vehicle headed straight for the tiger. Nero noticed this change of direction. The large hunter wasted no time in leaning out of the window with his gun and firing wildly. The bullets all struck the rocks around Sahbaar, who froze with fear. He had recognized the man and his stick, but when the stick made a sound, the tiger did not realize he was being shot at. The leader, jolted by the rifle firing right next to his head, slammed on the brakes. Before the angry man could yell at him, the large hunter took better aim and fired one more shot. It hit the rocks right above Sahbaar, causing several small stones to fall and bounce off the top of the tiger's head. This broke Sahbaar's trance, and he leaped away and scurried behind some larger rocks.

Nero couldn't believe his eyes. Something had caused those rocks to fall on his friend. It had happened right after the large man pointed his stick at the tiger and caused it to make the sky roar. Something was happening that the lion could not see. Suddenly, Nero was very frightened for his friend. He had been taught lions and tigers had no real predators. Now he realized this was not true.

The leader had resumed driving. As the Land Rover bounced across the field, he struggled to control the vehicle. Still, he found a way to reach back and repeatedly slap the large man in the head. "You idiot!" he cried. "If that cat would have fallen off those rocks, his coat would have been *ruined*! Besides, I want to take him alive, and you nearly made me go deaf!"

"Alive?" the bearded man questioned. "We don't have a cage!"

"We have nets," the man snapped back "and a lot of rope. I'm not going to waste time going back to town for a cage now." His voice softened. "We have to keep tracking this thing while we can. If we leave now and come back, it will disappear, trust me. We'll never find it. We should be able to get it back to town tied up. I'll pour some whiskey down its throat to knock it out if I have to." The two others grinned. They liked it when the boss was this way. It usually meant more work for them, but also more money.

The truck pulled up to the base of the rocks, and the large man jumped out. He helped the bearded man pass nets out of the side door, and they each slung a bundle onto their backs. The leader passed them both and began climbing up the rocky path. "Stay behind me," he told the others, "and be quiet! Maybe we can sneak right up on the thing!" Slowly, they crept along.

Nero was in a panic. The lion had learned enough about stalking prey to know Man was now hunting Sahbaar! He had to help his friend, but how? Then he saw Sahbaar appear at the top of the rock tower again.

The white and brown tiger was confused. After he had retreated from the falling rocks, he had looked around and then finally down. He blinked at the sight before him. It was the three hunters at the edge of his jungle! Sahbaar did not understand why they were there, or what the thing was that they were crawling out of. When they started up the rock path, he had a feeling they were responsible for the rockslide and were coming after him. Sahbaar had to hide quickly, and he looked around desperately. Luckily, he saw a small cave entrance tucked into the rocks.

On the other side of the field, Nero watched Sahbaar look around quickly, and then crouch down and suddenly seemed to disappear. The lion pulled his head back into the bushes, moved over to his left a bit, and then poked his head through again. From this angle, he could barely see the edge of a small dark spot on the rocks. Nero guessed it must be a small opening to a cave  The lion smiled. He remembered how, as cubs, he and his friend had spent many hours searching the other caves by the tiger family lair. Sahbaar was an expert at crawling through the tightest holes and sneaking around in the darkness. If anyone could hide from Man in a cave, it would be Sahbaar!

The leader came around a rock just in time to see the tiger's tail disappear into the hole. He told one, and then the other of his assistants to follow the tiger into the hole. "You're crazy!" the bearded one said, and his large friend nodded. "You don't pay us near enough to do something as crazy as that! You're such a tough guy, why don't you do it?!"

"Ah - um – ah," the boss stammered, searching for an excuse. "Well, then, we'll just wait 'em out. I've got nothing better to do." He motioned to the others to each stand on opposite sides of the hole with their nets ready. It wasn't long, though, before the two sat down on the rocks to wait instead. At first, the leader was upset, but soon he too had found a place to sit and wait. Nero chuckled. He knew Sahbaar could stay in that cave all day.

Fortunately, the tiger didn't have to. He knew these rocks well, and could crawl and climb through the network of caves until he came out in the back of his and Bahar's own lair. He surprised his uncle, who was just waking up from a nap. "Sahbaar, you look frightened. What is it?" he asked.

"Man has returned," Sahbaar said. "The hunters. They are on the rocks above us. I believe they are hunting me! We must flee before they come here and discover us and use their sky roar sticks!" The two cats bounded out of the cave and into the jungle. Their sudden exit from the lair startled Akoorah, who was napping on a low branch. She flew after the two until they stopped to rest and look around.

"Why do you run?" the bird questioned, landing on a tall stone.

"Man - is - hunting - Sahbaar" Bahar panted.

"One pointed his stick at me and caused rocks to fall on my head," Sahbaar added. "He was not even near me!"

"I think I figured out how they do this thing," the bird said. "One day, I saw the hyenas feasting on an antelope with no hide. I knew Man must have left it there. Suddenly, one of them began to choke. He finally spit out what looked like a small stone, only smoother and much harder. The others became more careful, and found more of the stones deep in the flesh. I believe the sticks Man points can somehow spit these stones faster than the wind, and harder than the stomp of a great elephant." These words frightened the two natural hunters. They crouched down in the bushes and waited for Man to come.

Meanwhile, up on the rocks, the leader was getting tired of waiting. He began yelling at the men again, demanding one or the other crawl into the darkness, and calling them chickens when they refused. When the large man told the leader he should do it, the man suddenly got quiet again. Muttering to himself, he looked around and finally found a very long stick. "Get ready," he warned the others. "He's going to come out mad!" Leaning away from the hole, and with his arm outstretched, he shoved the stick violently into the opening and stirred it around, ready at any moment to jump out of the way. When he didn't hit anything soft, he moved the stick harder. Suddenly, the long stick slipped out of his hand and, to everyone's amazement, disappeared completely into the hole! In disgust, the leader turned without a word and stomped off down the rock path. The other two looked at each other, shrugged their shoulders, and followed their leader. By the time the trio was near the bottom, the leader was no longer upset. "I've got a better idea," he said. "We'll set a trap with those nets."

"We'll have to do it tomorrow," the bearded man said, looking up. "It's starting to get dark." The others agreed and continued down to the truck.

Across the field, Nero was relieved to see they were leaving without Sahbaar. He did not understand why they wanted a tiger, but then again, it seemed they did not care what kind of animal they killed, or how many. The lion had a feeling they would not give up until his tiger friend was lying at their feet. Nero had to think of a way to help Sahbaar. He hurried back to the others to tell them what had happened.

Sahbaar and Bahar waited a long time in the bushes. They sent Akoorah flying all around to see where Man had gone. She was gone quite a while, searching all over. Finally, she returned to say she could not find them anywhere. She did not realize the three hunters had not gone back across the field, but had stayed in Sahbaar's jungle and had set up a camp far to the south, down by the river. Since they didn't know where these foes were, Sahbaar and Bahar decided it wasn't worth it to try and get back to the lair. Instead, they both climbed way up a huge tree. Up where the thick foliage would hide them from sight, they stretched out on thick limbs and were soon fast asleep.

A tree is fine for a tiger to nap in, but it is hard to sleep on a limb all night. Several times, the white tiger almost fell out of the tree. It was not much better for Bahar. For this reason, neither one got much sleep until the early morning. It was almost noon before they climbed down from their perch. Sahbaar looked around, then raised his head and sniffed the air. He had become familiar with the smell of Man, and it seemed to be in the air that morning. Bahar smelled it too, and asked Akoorah to fly up and see if they were around. She flew in great circles before returning with the news that she had not seen any of them. Both of the cats still felt uneasy as they began to look for some breakfast.

Finding food to hunt had become more difficult since Man had arrived. Sahbaar and Bahar were quite surprised, then, when they came through some bushes and almost fell over a large wild boar stretched out across the ground. Sahbaar backed off and then sniffed it suspiciously from a distance. "I think this was a Man kill," he said softly.

"How can it be?" Bahar questioned. "We heard no sky sounds today."

Sahbaar still had his doubts. "Man is much too clever not to have another way to hunt," he replied. The cat circled the dead animal. "See, look at the neck. I have never seen a wound so smooth and straight!" The animal was correct, for the leader of the hunters had slit the boar's neck with a sharp knife in order to be silent.

Bahar was very hungry. "I don't know," he said to Sahbaar. "It looks all right to me."

"Eat it if you wish," the other replied. "I don't want any of this kill."

Bahar was about to step forward, but then he stopped. "Perhaps you are right," he said. "Besides, we are hunters ourselves. No one has to get our food for us. Let the hyenas have this". Suddenly, they heard a noise and hid in the bushes. The large man and bearded man appeared. "So, they have not left," Bahar muttered.

"Darn!" said the bearded man. "Nothing yet!"

"I don't know," the large man replied, bending forward and squinting. "I think it may have nibbled on this leg."

"Where?" the other said, crowding close to his partner.

"There," the large man said, pointing. Just then, Sahbaar had an idea. He motioned for Bahar to follow him as he crept silently behind the men. Suddenly, Sahbaar leaped out, roaring and landed inches from them. Bahar followed, landing next to his nephew, and the two hunters screamed in fright and leaped forward. Sahbaar thought they would run away again, but he was astonished when there was suddenly a great commotion as if the ground was rising up. From under the foliage - and the boar - the net traps launched upward. In an instant, the two hunters and the boar were hanging from the trees in a gathered net.

The white and brown tiger jumped back in surprise. Confused by the sudden event, he and Bahar bounded back into the brush as the two trapped men began to shout for help. The cats watched from their hiding place as the leader appeared, slapped his forehead, and cut the two now humbled men down. He began to yell, and Sahbaar could tell by the tone of his voice that it was not good for them. The leader stormed off with the others following, heads down, leaving the boar and the nets behind them. Sahbaar and Bahar looked at each other for a few minutes, trying to figure out what had just happened. When they finally realized they had caused the men to get caught in their own trap, they both began to roll on the ground, roaring with laughter.

## CHAPTER FOUR
## FRIENDS TO THE RESCUE!

Far away in the other jungle, Nero and his friends were not laughing. The lion had spent the last evening telling his friends about seeing Sahbaar and the hunters, and the strange connection between the large man pointing his stick and the rocks falling on Sahbaar. He also told of the hunter's attempt to catch their friend. "We must help him!" Gahdar cried, stomping his feet excitedly. "If Man is as savage and uncaring a hunter as you say they are, then they will not think twice about killing Sahbaar."

"Yes, we must help him," Ahgrah added, "but how? We can't even go to where he is!"

"I've been thinking about that," Nero replied. "When it rains at night, and the wind is blowing, it gets cold in the treetops. I have seen the birds around our family lair hide under the thickest patches of leaves to stay warm."

"So?" Gahdar blurted. "What does that have to do with this problem?" "Well," Nero continued, "maybe if those birds hide, the border birds at the end of the jungle also hide."

Gahdar did not agree. "You're talking about the border birds. They are guards for the King! Do you think they would shirk their official duty just to keep from getting wet?"

Nero was confident. "I don't think they are as totally loyal as we are led to believe," he replied. "I have heard tell that lately many of them are not happy with my father because there are no birds in the Jungle Council. It would not surprise me if they picked comfort over duty."

"If they aren't watching when it rains," Ahgrah said, getting excited, "that means they would not see us sneak over to find Sahbaar!" Nero nodded, smiling.

"That would mean we have to be out in the rain ourselves!" Gahdar whined. "I'll get all wet!"

"What's wrong with that?" Ahgrah asked. "I'm out in the rain all the time! It's great!"

"That may be fine for a big water lizard," Gahdar replied playfully. Ahgrah swatted at the rhino with her tail.

"Can't you put up with a little discomfort for your friend Sahbaar?" Nero asked.

The rhino thought for a moment. "I suppose, but what are we going to do when we find him?"

Now it was Nero's turn to think. "I don't know," he said finally. "We will have to see what can be done at that time. So, will you come with me?"

"Yes!" Ahgrah cried enthusiastically, but Gahdar hesitated.

"Well, all right," the rhino said finally, and Nero smiled.

They agreed to meet near Nero's lair the first rainy night. A few days later, it rained all day. It was late in the afternoon when the rhino and crocodile met under a tree at nearly the same time. Nero was waiting, and he led the others off into the downpour. Gahdar whimpered all the way, but Ahgrah was enjoying herself. Unfortunately, just like before, the crocodile could only go a short way before the thick brush proved to be too great an obstacle. Nero reluctantly suggested that perhaps she should stay behind. "I care just as much about Sahbaar as you do," Ahgrah replied firmly, "and I really want to go help him." Nero understood but did not know how it would be possible. To search for paths to follow would take too long.

Suddenly, Gahdar had an idea. He found a slab of rock that the crocodile could crawl up onto which was almost level with his back. He then stood close to the edge so that Ahgrah could crawl right onto his back. "Climb on!" the rhino called to her. When she was settled, Gahdar stepped away and began to trudge off. "Come on," he called to Nero, who then bounded on ahead.

"You don't mind carrying me, do you?" Ahgrah asked meekly.

"Not at all," came the reply. "You are not heavy. Besides, you are helping to keep part of my back dry!"

The three friends trudged on. Now and then, Gahdar shook his head to shake off the loose drops of rain. Nero didn't seem to notice the weather, as his thoughts were with his tiger friend. The lion's mind was racing as he pushed through the wet foliage. Gahdar's concerns came back to him. He had no idea how he and his two friends could help the tiger. Nero had not forgotten what ruthless hunters Man were, and their strange sticks were certainly frightening. Would it really be possible for the animals to compete with these magical sticks and a moving lair? The cat began to shiver, more with worry than the cold. Still, he trudged on, determined to find a way to help.

At last, they reached the edge of the jungle. Nero looked up into the trees. Just as he had predicted, the border birds were nowhere to be seen. They were so well concealed that the trio was unable to locate even one feather among the swaying branches. "It looks like the birds won't be a problem," he told the others. "We should go on."

Gahdar was a bit reluctant to leave, as the thick clump of trees was the best rain protection they had had since they started. Just then, there was a flash of lightning and a loud crack of thunder, and the rain began to come down harder. "Oh, great!" Gahdar moaned. "I don't think I'll ever be dry again!"

"Come on," Nero urged. "I see a straight line without any bushes or rocks in the way that stretches all the way across the field. Let's just run across it. There are even thicker trees on the other side for you to stand under!"

This was enough to inspire the rhino. Gahdar began to charge down the gentle slope, forgetting about the crocodile on his back. After only a few bounces, Ahgrah suddenly flew off and thumped on the soft ground. Gahdar stopped immediately to apologize to his friend, but when he looked down, she wasn't there! He heard 'Whee!', and looked farther ahead. The unhurt Ahgrah was sliding down the hill, paddling her feet to skim across the rain-slicked grass! Relieved, Gahdar began to gallop after her. Nero bounded alongside both of them, and they all reached the other side at nearly the same time.

Gahdar and Ahgrah huddled beneath the trees, but the wind was so strong that it blew the rain at them from all sides. Nero did some scouting and found a cave entrance. "I have found a cave!" he called, returning. "I think we should sleep there, and then search for Sahbaar in the morning." The others quickly nodded, and the three wearily travelers trudged to the dark cave. Gahdar and Ahgrah plopped down and were asleep in moments, but Nero lay thinking. They had done it! They had outsmarted the border birds, and come to their friend's rescue. The lion could not wait to see his furry friend again. He hoped they weren't too late.

Sahbaar woke with a strange feeling. He knew something was different even before he opened his eyes. The tiger raised his head and looked around sleepily. The scene at the front of the cave confused him. He blinked and squinted. He could swear he saw his old friends lying together asleep. "Nero!" he called out. "Nero, is that you?"

The lion woke up suddenly, looking around. He was sure he heard his friend's voice, but there was no one there. Had he been dreaming? He heard his name again and looked up to a rock ledge near the back of the cave. As Nero and Sahbaar's eyes met, they both leaped to their feet. Sahbaar scrambled to the cave floor, as Nero raced to greet him. Howling with delight, the two cats began to tumble and wrestle just like in their younger days. "Ouch, ooh, the rocks!" Nero winced, and Sahbaar stopped. As soon as he did, his grinning friend rolled over and pounced again.

The noise woke Gahdar and Ahgrah, who sat smiling. When the wrestlers finally took a break, the white tiger greeted his other friends warmly. "Ahgrah, I hardly recognize you! Soon you will be bigger than your mother! Gahdar, your horn is huge!"

"I see you still have your special coloring," the rhino replied. "To think I was frightened of you once. Now I think your coat makes you look so powerful and majestic."

"Yes, I agree," Ahgrah said, and Nero nodded.

Sahbaar was embarrassed. "It's still just the same old me," he said quietly, looking at the cave floor.

Then Gahdar suddenly became very serious. "Sahbaar, I am so sorry about what happened. I never meant to expose your secret and get you banished," he wailed.

Sahbaar patted Gahdar's shoulder. "It is all right, my friend. I'm sure Rahshar would have found out eventually. At least I can now truly be myself. Besides, if this hadn't happened, I never would have met my uncle." Gahdar looked at him strangely. "Oh, my uncle!" the tiger exclaimed, glancing over at the other, who was quietly watching them from his ledge. "Where are my manners? Let me introduce you all to my Uncle Bahar, who helped me greatly when I first came here."

The old tiger stood up slowly and began to make his way down to the others. As he grew nearer, they all noticed his leg, but only for a moment. Sahbaar introduced each of his friends, and at their request, Bahar told them his own banishment story. When Bahar finished, he excused himself to go get a drink from the rainwater pool. Sahbaar took that opportunity to question his friends more. "So, how did you all get here?" he began excitedly. "Has Rahshar changed his mind? Can I go back to my parents?"

"No," Nero answered sadly. "You are still banished. We had to sneak over here."

"It was such a plan!" Gahdar broke in, trying to lift the mood. "Nero is so clever. He had us wait for a rainy, windy night, so the border birds would be hiding instead of keeping watch. Then, we just ran right across the field!"

"Why did you all risk so much to come here?" Sahbaar questioned. "Surely, you could be in serious trouble as we speak."

Ahgrah, who had been very quiet, suddenly remarked, "It's all right.

We are all old enough to be away from our parents without them wondering about us. We have been away from them for many days before. Besides, the old jungle is very large. We could be anywhere. No one will think we have come over here." The others nodded in agreement.

"All right, you are safe," Sahbaar agreed, "but that doesn't answer why you came."

This time Nero spoke up as Bahar rejoined the group. "Man has come into our jungle. They are three hunters. We have seen their wasteful hunting ways."

"We also have seen this behavior," Bahar replied. "Sahbaar and I refuse to eat their kill."

"I was hiding at the edge of the old jungle the day they came after Sahbaar," Nero continued. "They pointed their sticks that make the sky sounds at you."

"We have seen them use the sticks also," Sahbaar confirmed. "Our friend Akoorah the bird told us some hyenas found small, very hard stones deep in Man's kill. She thinks their sticks spit these stones very hard and fast, and that is how they bring down the prey." The others were all disturbed by this news.

"These creatures are truly dangerous," Nero remarked. "That is why we felt we had to come and help you. Man has hunted you once; I'm sure they will try again."

"They already have," Bahar replied. "With some kind of vine web." He told the others all about the trap the hunters had set. When he told how Sahbaar managed to snare them in their own nets, the three animals howled with laughter.

"It sounds like they are not so mighty without their sticks," Gahdar observed. "What if we tried to get the sticks away from them?"

"That is a great idea!" Sahbaar agreed, and the rhino beamed. "It won't be easy, but we must take their sticks away. Then perhaps we can chase them off."

"We must find them first," Nero said. "Do you know where they are?" Sahbaar shook his head. "We have been having trouble keeping track of them."

The lion thought a moment. "Let's all go out and listened for the growl of their moving lair. That is how I found them before."

Sahbaar looked at his friend strangely. "Moving lair? Is that what I saw in the field that day?"

"Yes," Gahdar interrupted, eager to be able to share more information.

"Man has a large lair that they all crawl into, and then the lair carries them like a mother might carry its young." Bahar stared in awe at this information, and Sahbaar smiled, letting his friend continue. "It can move very fast, and tromp down small bushes like the elephant," the rhino continued eagerly to his captive audience. "Though we have never seen it swim or climb a tree."

"Elephants can't climb trees!" Ahgrah teased, and Gahdar glared at her.

"I have a safer way to find Man," Sahbaar said. He walked to the cave entrance and called for Akoorah. When the bird appeared and landed, Sahbaar introduced her to everyone. Then he told her of their plan and asked her to fly up and try to locate Man again.

"I would be happy to help any way I can," the bird replied, and took off. As they relaxed and waited for the bird's return, Bahar began telling stories of the old jungle when he and Nero's father were only cubs. Even Sahbaar listened in silent wonder.

After a while, Akoorah returned. "I have found Man, just to the south. They are digging a large hole! There is a path you can follow." With the bird in the lead, the group of animals marched out of the cave single file and went to find Man again.

It wasn't long before they were there. Sure enough, the large man and bearded man were both digging a hole, using sticks with strangely flattened ends. The large man was making very angry noises at the leader, who sat watching them. Now and then, the bearded man would also make a few angry sounds.

"Tell me again, why we are doing this?" the large man asked.

"Well," the leader began, "Our last trap didn't work because you two idiots sprang the thing yourselves before the tiger even had a chance." The large man was going to protest, but the leader held up his hand to silence him. "We're going to give that tiger another shot at getting some free grub. This time, we're going to try a gazelle."

"How will he know it's here?" the bearded man questioned.

"He found the boar, didn't he? He must spend all day looking for food. Trust me, he will find it, and it's not like we have a time limit. I will wait a month for that prize to come around!"

"Well, I'm getting tired of doing all the work around here!" the large man snapped at the leader. "You know, you aren't any better than we are!"

"Yeah!" the bearded man added. "This was your idea. Why do we have to do all the work?"

The leader had ignored these kinds of remarks as the men dug, but now he grew tired of them. "Listen, you apes!" he shouted suddenly. "I'm the brains in this group, and I have to save my energy for thinking. You don't know how to do anything! If I left it up to you that white tiger hide would be worthless, 'cause it would be full of bullet holes! If it weren't for me, you two idiots would have been caught a long time ago! Either that or you would be broke and starving! So quit your whining, and keep digging!"

The large man and the bearded man knew the leader was right. With a loud sigh, they continued working on the hole. Satisfied, the leader began looking through some papers. Sahbaar and the others watched the hole get wider and deeper. Meanwhile, Nero tried to see where the sky sound sticks were. He could not see them, so he guessed Man was keeping them in the moving lair. He told the others about his hunch.

"Someone has to go into the lair to get them," Sahbaar said quietly. "Akoorah, could you do it?"

The bird looked thoughtful. "I don't think I'm strong enough to lift even one," she said.

"I will do it," Nero said, "but I will have to get past Man first."
"That is no problem," Bahar whispered. "Man scares more easily than young gazelle! We will all jump out at them, and when they run, Nero can go to the lair." It was agreed. When the lion was ready, the rest of the animals burst from the bushes, making as much noise as possible. The large man screamed, the bearded man hollered, and they fell over each other and their shovels trying to crawl out of the hole. The leader fell off his chair, throwing papers into the air, then scrambled to his feet and dashed into the jungle after the other two. Nero bounded over to the lair and crawled through an open window. It was very dark and full of strange smells. In the dim light, the lion finally found Man's sticks.

At first, Nero wasn't sure how to pick one up. Then he remembered Man's paws holding the stick in various ways, so he felt it would be safe. He bent his head forward and very gently bit down on the center of one stick. Cautiously raising his head, he began to try and turn so he could go back out the hole he had come in. The ends of the stick bounced off of various objects as the lion struggled to keep his grip. Suddenly, the stick popped out of his mouth and fell. Nero ducked his head quickly, but nothing happened. The determined beast picked up the stick again and then realized it would not fit through the hole this way. Laying it down gently, he began to push at it with his paws to turn it sideways to the hole. Having accomplished this, he realized he would not be able to pick it up and step through the hole the same way. He tried to pick it up by the end, but it was too heavy to lift it that way. Frustrated, he began to swat at the stick without thinking. The gun went off suddenly, shattering the windshield of the truck completely. Nero wasted no time in leaping through the large hole and following his friends into the jungle.

The frightened band ran all the way back to the tiger lair. When they were all safe inside, Sahbaar asked, "Nero, are you all right?" The shaken lion nodded.

"What happened?" Ahgrah asked.

"I could not get the stick out of the lair," the lion explained. "It was very hard for me to carry. It would be much easier if my paws were like Man's.

"Yes, that would be easier," Sahbaar agreed, "but none of us has paws like Man."

The animals all stopped to ponder this. Then Gahdar's head snapped up, and his eyes grew wide. "No, none of *us* has paws like Man, but I know who does. Cheerah!"

"Yes, Cheerah!" Ahgrah agreed excitedly. "She can get the sticks!"

"Do you think she will she do it?" Sahbaar broke in. "She always tells us how she is a friend to Man. Would she be willing to go against them?"

"I think she might," Nero replied. "These hunters we saw disturbed her greatly."

"The best way to find out," Bahar spoke up, "is to have her come here and talk with us."

"But how will she get here?" Ahgrah asked the others.

"Cheerah is very clever," Sahbaar replied. "She will think of a way to get past the border birds. Could you go find her tomorrow?" he asked Akoorah. The bird nodded.

Meanwhile, the hunters had gradually made their way back to the camp. The trio peeked from behind trees to make sure the animals were gone before coming out. The leader was very angry. He barked at the others to get back to their digging and then began to examine the Land Rover. Before the man had run off, he had seen Nero climb into the vehicle. "That lion crawled in here on purpose!" he wondered out loud as he looked around. "What was he trying to do?"

"I'll tell you one thing," the large man puffed as he shoveled. "There's something screwy about those animals. That old tiger travels with the white and brown one."

"Plus this time, there were others with them," the bearded man replied, "including that lion!"

"Plus they keep showing up to mess up our traps!" the large man said more excitedly.

"As if they know what we're doing, and are trying to wreck it!" the bearded man almost shouted. The two stopped and stared at each other as if each couldn't believe they were actually agreeing about something.

For once, the leader didn't disagree or tell them they were stupid. Their comments had made him think. "You know, boys, I think you're right," he said almost gently. Now the other two looked at him in surprise. "We're going to have to watch out for those critters," he continued. "No dumb beast is going to outwit me! Why don't you stop now, and help me clean up this glass? Then we'll quit for the night." The two men gladly threw down their shovels and crawled out of the deepening hole.

Early the next morning, Sahbaar woke his friends. Gahdar and Ahgrah told the bird Akoorah where they would most likely find Cheerah the gibbon. After Akoorah left, the animals ate again and then waited. To their surprise, the bird returned in a very short time. "Did you have any trouble getting past the border birds?" Nero asked.

"No, they didn't seem to notice me," the bird said, almost offended. "I've found your friend where you said she would be. She is very nice, and would like to help you very much."

"Did she say when she might get here?" Gahdar asked anxiously. "Very soon," the bird answered. "We are all supposed to wait high up on the rocks where we have a good view of the field."

The animals were all confused. Was the gibbon really planning on crossing the field in the bright light of day? They all had no idea what to expect. Sahbaar knew the rocks well, and he found a place with a clump of bushes his friends could hide in so the border birds would not see them. The animals all settled down and waited. They did not have to wait long. Across the field, almost exactly where Nero and the others had come out, they spotted some movement in the bushes. Then Cheerah's head popped out, and she looked around for the border birds.

She saw Sahbaar up on the rocks then and managed to sneak a hand wave before disappearing again. There were more brush movements, and then some of the bushes seemed to move forward. Sure enough, a small 'bush' came out of the clump until it was sitting alone. Then, as the others watched in amazement, it began to move forward again. The 'bush' would rise up a few inches, move forward a foot or so quickly, then stop and sink next to other bushes. Sahbaar and his friends were quite amused, because each time the bush rose and moved forward, they could see Cheerah's feet!

"She doesn't really think she's going to make it, does she?" Bahar asked. "The border birds will notice her for sure!"

"Well," Sahbaar said with a smile, "she's made it so far. I guess those birds are a lot more foolish than we thought."

"Oh, yes," Akoorah agreed. "They aren't the best choice for guards, I can tell you that!"

The group watched with delight as Cheerah zigzagged across the field, never stopping next to a bush for more than a few minutes. Above her head, the birds circled slowly but never suspected a thing. At last, the gibbon was in the forbidden jungle, and the others hurried down to meet her. They all praised her for her cleverness and bravery. After meeting Bahar, she was eager to know how she could help her old friend Sahbaar.

"Nero tells me you have seen Man and his strange sticks, and have heard of his hunting ways," Sahbaar began.

"Yes," the gibbon replied solemnly. "It is very disturbing how these Man are such wasteful hunters. This is also quite surprising. There are no hunters at the Man lair I visit, and they are all very kind to the animals."

"It is worse than you imagine," Gahdar broke in. "Now Man is hunting Sahbaar!"

This upset Cheerah as much as it had upset the others. "Is this what you wish me to help you with?" she asked in a small, timid voice.

"It won't be so bad," Nero reassured her. "We have it all planned out. We will all go to their moving Man lair. You will hide near it in the bushes. The rest of us will leap out at them and chased them off. Then, while we keep them away, you sneak into the lair and take all the sticks." Cheerah did not look convinced.

"We have tried this before," Sahbaar continued. "It will be easy!"

"If it is so easy, why haven't you succeeded?" the gibbon protested.

"Because we need you," Nero took over. "I tried, but I had to pick up the sticks with my mouth. This was very difficult. Your paws are just like Man's. You can pick up and carry the sticks like they do. When they carry the sticks, it seems very safe."

Cheerah thought about it for a while. "Well, if you really need me, and it is something I can do, then I am happy to help. I just hope you are right about all of this!"

"Let's go right now," Nero said. "I don't want to waste another minute!"

## CHAPTER FIVE
## A BOLD PLAN

On a hunch, the group traveled back to the place they had seen Man the day before. Sure enough, there they were, in nearly the same spot. As Sahbaar and Bahar peeked through the bushes, they noticed that the moving lair now sat further away from a small clearing, behind some tall bushes. Something else was different, though. It took Sahbaar a few minutes to figure it out. The large hole Man had been digging the day before had disappeared! What the animals did not realize is that the large man and bearded man had risen early to finish digging it, and had now just barely finished covering it with loose foliage over sticks they had laid across the opening.

The leader had been waiting for the tiger to arrive, armed with one of the rifles, which was hidden at his side just in case he needed it. As his gaze drifted over to the covered pit, he suddenly realized that they had forgotten the 'bait'. "Hey, idiot!" he called to whichever man would answer, "You forgot to get the gazelle!"

"Do we have to remember everything?" the large man barked back. "I thought you were the 'brains'! You're supposed to be in charge of stuff like that!"

The leader was about to yell back when he heard rustling in the bushes. "Quiet!" he hissed to the others, "and don't move!"

"What is it, boss?" the bearded man whispered back.

"I think the tiger is here," came the reply, "or something. There in the bushes right in front of you! Just stay where you are, you two, and don't move!"

"Ahh, we don't have any guns," the bearded man hissed back.

"Just trust me," the leader said.

"Oh, boy, I hope he knows what he's doing," the large man replied fearfully.

Sahbaar motioned to the right, where a bit of the Land Rover was visible. "There is the lair, Cheerah. When we leap out and frighten them, you run and climbed in as fast as you can. Pull out all the sticks you see and hide them under the thick thorn bush there." The gibbon nodded nervously. Sahbaar took a deep breath. "All right, let's go!" he whispered to the others. As before, they burst out of the bushes, making as much noise as they could.

At that point, things happened quickly. The large man and the bearded man jumped in fright but did not run off. That's because they were standing on the other side of the hole. As Sahbaar and Bahar landed in front of them, they felt through and into the pit. Somehow Nero, who had jumped a moment later, managed to push harder and jumped over the hole. He brushed against the bearded man who fell into a bush, then scrambled to his feet and ran off. Confused at where the two tigers had gone, Nero stood and looked around. When his eyes met the large man's, the frightened hunter screamed and ran off also. Nero chased after them. Luckily, the leader didn't have a chance to fire at the lion.

Gahdar had remained in the bushes because he was not good at leaping. He had seen the two tigers fall into the pit, and he decided to run around the hole at the leader. Before he got halfway around the pit, the leader suddenly raised his rifle. Gahdar gasped, stopped, and closed his eyes. Just as the leader was pulling the trigger, Ahgrah, who had dashed out ahead of her friend, whipped her tail around and knocked the hunter's feet out from under him. The gun tipped upward and went off as he fell, sending leaves showering down. Gahdar opened his eyes, saw he was all right, turned, and galloped off in the opposite direction. The hunter had not dropped the gun when he fell, and he quickly got to his knees and prepared to fire again at the retreating rhino. Ahgrah slapped him again, this time in the side, nearly knocked him into the hole. Yelling in fright, he had to drop the gun in order to hang onto the edge.

Meanwhile, Sahbaar and Bahar had gotten up and looked around. They were shaken but not hurt. As the leader's legs and torso swung into the pit, Sahbaar roared in anger. The usually tough leader began to whimper as he pawed at the ground. Finally, he crawled out and reached for his rifle, but a third slap from the crocodile's tail sent it flying into the bushes by the Land Rover.

Gahdar had heard the leader's yell and had come back. Peeking through the bushes, he saw the only ones there were Ahgrah and the leader, who was lying on the ground staring at her in fright. Seeing the leader no longer had his stick, the rhino bravely returned, determined to free Sahbaar and Bahar. Gahdar saw a short thick tree near the hole and decided to push it in so they could climb up and out. "Sahbaar, Bahar, moved to the side," he shouted, and began to butt the tree with his head.

The screams and shouts of the other two hunters had died down after they had run off, and for the moment, the only sound was the steady thump of Gahdar's head against the tree. Soon the two missing men were heard once again. This time the sounds of fear were replaced by shouts of anger.

Nero had chased them off, but as they reappeared, it was the men chasing Nero. The large man was tired of animals chasing him, and in desperation, he had grabbed a dead tree limb from the ground, turned, and shook it at the lion. Nero stopped. He wasn't sure if this was another of the special sticks or not. The bearded man saw this and picked up a large stick also. Nero decided not to find out if they were sky noise sticks or not, and he turned and ran back to the others. The lion paced himself and once again leaped over the hole, running off into the jungle. The two men stopped at the edge of the pit and shook their sticks at him.

The leader and Ahgrah had been staring at each other this whole time, the man in fear, and the crocodile in uncertainty. When the other men ran up, Ahgrah looked at them, and the leader suddenly leaped up and made a dash for the Land Rover.

While all this was going on, Cheerah had crawled through the windshield frame of the vehicle and had begun to look for the sticks. Quickly locating them, she carefully lifted the first and carried it to the window. The gibbon was about to toss it out under the bushes when she remembered that it had made its sound when Nero had just hit it. Cheerah decided to carry the stick out instead. When it was safely under the bush, she quickly went back for another. She was pushing the third rifle into the underbrush when the leader fired his rifle. This caused her to hide near the same bush. When the leader's rifle flew into the bushes in front of her, Cheerah quickly grabbed it and placed it with the others. She had gone back into the vehicle to search for more when the leader approached suddenly. Seeing the small animal in the vehicle, his confidence return. "Get out of here!" he yelled, waving his arm at the gibbon. "You don't belong in here!" Cheerah stayed just out of his reach, screeching wildly. With one eye, she looked for more sticks, even as the leader started to crawl in after her.

"I'll show you!" he growled, as he reached over and suddenly pulled out a large handgun. Cheerah could see it was not like the other sticks, but she didn't like the way he was pointing it at her. Just then, she saw another long stick and grabbed it. As she spun around with the weapon, the butt hit a large can of used motor oil that the large man had left inside the vehicle. The force of the impact caused the cover to pop off, and grimy oil splashed onto the rifle and the hunter, too. As he grabbed at the container with his free hand, the frightened gibbon scurried out the side window. She was going to take this stick back to the tiger lair for Nero to look at, but it was too slippery with oil to run with. She tossed it under the bushes with the others and ran off into the woods screeching wildly.

"Come back with that!" the leader cried from half inside the Land Rover. He was about to fire the pistol when there was a loud crash behind him. He hit the back of his head on the vehicle's roof as he tried to straighten up quickly.

Running back to the pit, he saw an incredible sight. Gahdar had succeeded in pushing the tree over into the hole! Sahbaar and Bahar quickly ran up the trunk and out of their prison. The two other hunters, now confronted by these cats, dropped their sticks and ran off screaming again. The leader was furious, and he aimed his pistol right at the white and brown tiger. He was so upset he had forgotten about Ahgrah. She took careful aim, and this time succeeded in knocking him completely into the hole with her tail. The pistol flew out of his hand and right over the group, who watched its flight. The weapon came down hard on a bunch of rocks, and several pieces broke off. Sahbaar had seen Cheerah run off, and hoped she had completed her task. He turned and headed back towards the tiger cave, with the others following. Nero stopped a moment to sniff at the broken pistol and nudge it with his paw. Another piece fell off, and the cat snorted and hurried to catch up with the others.

Back in the tiger lair, they found Cheerah waiting. The animals all relaxed after their great confrontation with Man. "That hole was definitely meant to trap you two," Nero said.

"It was a good thing that we had someone like Gahdar to free you," Ahgrah said proudly about her friend.

The rhino lowered his head modestly, then raised it and quickly added, "and I was lucky to have Ahgrah there. She saved my life, and saved us all!" Now the crocodile smiled proudly.

"You all did an excellent job in defeating Man," Bahar beamed. "Sahbaar, you have some truly great friends!" Then everyone began to comment at once about the brave things each of the others had done. This included much praise for Cheerah.

"I found four sticks in the lair," the gibbon said proudly, "and another came flying over on its own!

"That was thanks to Ahgrah's tail" Gahdar replied proudly. The crocodile smiled at her friend.

"I hid them deep in the thorn bushes," Cheerah continued. "I would have carried the last one back here right away, but Man was chasing me, so I hid it with the others instead."

"We can get them tomorrow before the sky gets light," Nero said.

"Sahbaar and Bahar and I will guard the path while Cheerah carries them back."

"What will we do with them when we get them here?" Ahgrah asked.

"I have been thinking about that," Sahbaar replied. "You saw how the small stick Man had broken when it hit those rocks. If we drop the large sticks onto the rocks from a high place, they might break also." With this new plan in place, the animals all suddenly felt very tired. They decided to go to sleep early so they would be fresh when they went to retrieve the sticks.

Back at the pit, the large man and bearded man had finally wandered back slowly, looking around nervously. "Are they gone?" the large man called to the leader as he peeked from behind a tree.

"They're gone," the leader snarled as he pawed at the bushes. "Come over here, you scared babies, and help me look for the rifles. While those others were keeping us busy, a stupid gibbon climbed into the Rover and stole 'em!"

"I told you!" the large man said. "Those animals are smart. I think *they* are trying to get rid of *us*!" The bearded man nodded excitedly in agreement.

"You know, I have to agree with you about that, too," the leader said in a calmer voice. "I'm not about to give up, though. The stakes are even greater now." He looked at the two others, who just stared back with blank faces. "Didn't you see that rhino?" he hinted. The two men just shook their heads, still puzzled. The leader slapped his forehead. "I don't believe this. You call yourselves poachers? Don't you know anything?"

"Enough with the riddles!" the large man spouted. "Tell us, already!"

"That rhino had just one horn. Do you know what kind of a trophy that would make?" the leader said excitedly. "Just like that white and brown tiger, one horn rhino heads are worth a lot of money!"

"Um...ah...we know that!" the bearded man stammered, trying to cover his ignorance. The large man just nodded vigorously. The leader glared at the both of them.

"So we are going to do whatever it takes to get that tiger and rhino," the leader continued, "and if the others get in the way, we'll take care of 'em!"

"Now you're talking!" the large man shouted. "Let's find those guns!" The next morning, well before the sun had risen, the animals ventured out of the cave. Akoorah flew to the pit to see where Man was. She heard strange growling noises coming from a new, smaller lair off beyond the other side of the moving one. Landing by the tent opening, she peeked inside and saw all three of the hunters snoring away. "They are still sleeping" she called to the others as she flew up. "If you hurry, it may be easier. I will sit in the tree by their sleeping lair entrance, and if they wake, I will warn you." The three cats set off. It had been decided that Gahdar and Ahgrah would stay at the cave and guard the rifles as Cheerah brought them.

Sahbaar, Nero, and Bahar spaced themselves equally along the path and stepped back into the brush. Cheerah went all the way to the hiding place and felt under the bush. To her relief, Man had barely searched for the weapons the day before and had not found the sticks. She pulled one out and began lumbering down the path with it, trying to be quiet. Each cat watched her pass by. Soon, she was at the cave, and she gently set the weapon down just inside the doorway. "Four more to go!" she told the two guards, and then headed off.

The second and third rifles were moved without a problem, but when she came back for the fourth one, Akoorah flew over and landed next to her. "Man is moving! Man is moving!" she whispered excitedly, flapping her wings. "You must run! You must hide!" Cheerah was determined to move all the sticks first. She slid one out slowly, picked it up, and began to step gently down the path.

Just then, the leader came out of the tent, just on the other side of the Land Rover. "Come on, you two!" he shouted. "Get out here! We have to find those guns!"

The large man came out, yawning and scratching his belly. "What about breakfast?" he asked sleepily.

"I'll 'breakfast' you!" his boss growled. "Let's get going!" The bearded man joined them.

Cheerah froze as she heard Man begin to move. The leader went to the Land Rover and climbed in to get something. The vehicle creaked and groaned as he moved around inside. The large man and bearded man then began to leisurely search the bushes, moving slowly away from the truck. Cheerah thought if she tried to hide she would be discovered, and so she began to step down the path very gently. After what seemed like hours, she crept past Sahbaar, who nodded silently. By the time she passed Nero she was feeling better, and Bahar was far from Man, so at that point she just hurried back to the cave as fast as she could.

"What's wrong?" Gahdar asked, sensing Cheerah's uneasiness.

"Man has come out of his lair, and I almost didn't make it back with this stick. There is one left which I would really like to get, but I don't know if it is possible."

"Sahbaar and the others are still on the trail. Maybe you should ask them," Ahgrah suggested.

The gibbon scampered off and quickly snuck back to Sahbaar. "Man is moving around. Do you think I should try for the last stick?" she whispered to the cat.

"Yes," came the reply. "If we leave even one of them with Man, it will be a bad thing. Take the last one right in front of Man, if you have to. With no sticks to protect them, the three of us can surely frighten them away if they come after you."

The gibbon nodded and was off. She got back to the bush just as the bearded man was reaching under it from the other side. Cheerah and the hunter both grabbed the rifle at the same time, one at either end. "I got one!" the bearded man called out, and Cheerah began to panic. She grabbed her end with both hands and began to pull. The bearded man felt this, drop to his knees, and grabbed with both hands also. "Help!" he yelled. "Something's got the other end! Help!"

The leader flew out of the Land Rover and dropped to his knees next to the other, trying to find a place to grab on. Then he decided to run around to the other side, and find out who was fighting them. He was just getting up when the large man ran over. The large man tripped on a vine and fell onto the others. The bearded man lost his grip, and the rifle flew out the other side, knocking the gibbon over. She quickly got up, grabbed the weapon by the end, and gallop down the path, dragging it behind her.

"You idiot!" the leader screamed, pushing the large man off of him and leaping to his feet. "He had a rifle, and you made him lose it!"

"Are you sure it was a rifle?" the embarrassed large man said defensively.

"Oh, yeah," the bearded man said. "At least I think it was. It had some kind of oil on it," he added, wiping his hands on the grass.

"The oil that monkey knocked over!" the leader snapped. "He stashed the rifles under there!"

"Yep," the bearded man confirmed, moving the branches so he could see underneath. "It looks pretty matted down. They must have all been there, but they're not there now."

"I know that, stupid!" the leader shouted. "That blasted ape took 'em all!"

"What are we going to do without guns?" the large man asked. "I'm not going after that tiger and his buddies without one!"

"We gotta find that monkey," the leader said, calm again. "Start lookin'!" The trio began to walk around with their heads tilted back, searching the treetops for the creature and their guns.

Cheerah was out of breath when she dragged the last rifle into the lair. Sahbaar wanted to make sure Man had not followed the gibbon back. He crept back to the Man camp until he could peek through the long grass at them. Nero and Bahar had the same idea, and soon they joined the other cat.

"What are they doing?" Nero whispered.

"They must be looking for Cheerah," Bahar guessed. "I'm glad they didn't catch her."

"I have an idea," Sahbaar said. "Bahar, you go back and ask Cheerah to take all the sticks to the top of our rock tower, on the other end, away from the field. Show her the way, and have the others help you. When you are done, send Akoorah back to tell us."

"What are you planning?" Bahar asked.

"I think we should make sure Man knows we are serious," Sahbaar replied. "We will break their sticks in front of them!"

Bahar crept back to the cave while Sahbaar and Nero kept watching Man. The large man and bearded man kept their eyes skyward, each wanting to be the first to spot the gibbon. They kept bumping into trees and each other, and twice they almost knocked the leader down. It was all the two cats could do to keep from laughing.

After a while, Akoorah flew up and landed on the bush Sahbaar and Nero were behind. "Cheerah and the others are ready," she said breathlessly. "The sticks are all at the top." With that, the white and brown cat rose and leisurely wandered out onto the path, and Nero followed. It took a few minutes for the men to notice them. The cats pretended not to see them and began to walk back to the tower. Staying a safe distance back, the leader motion for the others to be quiet and follow him as he crept behind the two cats. When they all reached the path winding up the towers, Sahbaar suddenly began to sprint, and Nero followed him around the corner. The men ran up to the path but weren't sure where their prey had gone. Then suddenly, Cheerah began to screech from the top of the tower.

The three hunters looked up at the gibbon. Cheerah put on a real show, dancing around and sticking her tongue out at the men. Angered, the leader took a few quick steps up the path, but just then Nero came down around the corner and roared loudly. The three hunters froze, and Nero took a step or two back and lay down in the middle of the path. He looked up at the monkey, and ignoring their instincts to not take their eyes off a wild animal, the three men looked up again. It was like they knew the gibbon was about to do something. As if on cue, the gibbon high above them produced a rifle and began to wave it over her head wildly. The hunters all held their breaths. Then, with an even wilder screech, Cheerah hurled the rifle down at the rocks below.

"Noooo!" the leader yelled, and the weapon hit the rocks hard and broke into several pieces. Since the other men's pistols were back at the camp, there wasn't much he could do. He told the large man to run back and get his gun, but when Nero saw him pointing in that direction, he stood and roared again. The leader slowly put his hand back down. Cheerah danced wildly in circles, and then produced another rifle. Once again, the leader took a step forward, but Nero roared once more. The second rifle shattered on the rocks, and Cheerah raised a third. The leader ran around the base of the tower, looking for another way up. There was none. Then the crazed man actually stood directly below the gibbon and looked up, as if he was ready to catch the weapon before it too was smashed. Cheerah saw this and threw the rifle with even more force. The leader had to dive out of the way to avoid being killed.

All this time, the large man and bearded man just stood with gaping mouths, not believing the deliberate show that was being played out in front of them. They were ready to run if the lion even twitched. After his brush with death, the leader walked back and stood humbly with the others, helplessly watching as the last two rifles were destroyed. He looked up at Cheerah, who was grinning proudly. Then Sahbaar appeared next to the gibbon and began to stare at the leader. The leader became tense, and his arms began to quiver as his anger grew. In sheer desperation, he picked up rocks and tried to throw them at the cat, which of course was well out of reach. As Sahbaar continued to stare, the rocks bounced off the tower and flew back at the men, who had to dodge them. One stone even hit the leader in the shoulder, but he ignored it and suddenly threw a rock at Nero. The cat quickly dodged the shot by leaping around the corner. Totally frustrated, the leader spun around and stomped back into the jungle to the Land Rover. His two assistants followed him, not daring to say a word.

After waiting to make sure they had left, Nero went to the top of the tower to join all his friends. The sun had warmed all the flat rocks on the field side of the tower nicely, and everyone stretched out to relax and enjoy their success. It wasn't long before they heard the growl of the Man lair, and soon it appeared and began to cross the field. To the animal's delight, it did not return to the other jungle again but turned north. This seemed to show that Man was finally leaving the jungle lands for good. All the friends cheered at how they had driven Man away. Sahbaar was not as excited as the others. He had an uneasy feeling that Man would return.

As the cheering died down, Cheerah suddenly became alarmed. "Look," she said, pointing across the field. The border birds were all flying in circles around the trees, squawking loudly.

"Down, everyone!" Sahbaar called out. "Hide!" Everyone ducked behind the large rocks. In their effort to defeat Man, they had forgotten all about the winged sentinels. Now their jubilation may have attracted the birds.

"Do you think they saw us?" Gahdar whispered nervously.
"I hope not," Sahbaar said. "I don't know for sure."

"There is one way to find out," Akoorah replied. "Go ask them!" In an instant, she was off, and soon she landed across the field in a tree. All the border birds landed near her, but it was too far away for Sahbaar and the others to hear anything.

"It's all my fault," Cheerah moaned. "I was jumping around and dancing like a fool just now!"

"It's not your fault!" Ahgrah comforted her friend. "We were all excited. Besides, I don't care if I get in trouble anyhow. I'm so glad I came to help my friend." All the others agreed and decided they would face any punishment ahead of them with pride, for they had done the honorable thing. Sahbaar humbly thanked them all. With that, they all turned their attention back to the border birds and waited for them to come and demand they return to Rahshar. Then, an odd thing happened. All the border birds took off as one flock, but instead of flying towards the group of friends, they flew back into their old jungle.

"They must be going to get Rahshar first," Gahdar said, confused. When the birds were out of sight, Akoorah rose and quickly flew back to the others.

"I think I fooled them," she said breathlessly as she landed. "When I asked what the fuss was all about, they told me Rahshar had a feeling a certain rhino, crocodile, lion, and gibbon might try to see Sahbaar, and he noticed they had been missing for a few days. The birds have been told to look for you and have been searching. They said they did see you just now, but I asked them to describe who they were looking for, and their description was really rather vague. I told them I had seen all of you on the far side of your old jungle, and they went to investigate."

Sahbaar looked at Akoorah suspiciously, and the bird knew what her friend was going to say. "I didn't really lie," she reassured the tiger. "I just didn't say *which* jungle I had seen all of you on the far side of." The others chuckled at the bird's cleverness. "Each one wanted to be the one to locate you," Akoorah continued. "So they all flew off without leaving any guards behind! They really are quite foolish."

The animals all thanked the bird in a chorus of voices. "There is no time for that now," Akoorah urged. "If you go now, you can run right back across the field. You must hurry, though. The border birds fly fast, and they will be back soon."

The animals all made their way down the rock tower and out to the edge of the field. Suddenly it was time to say goodbye. "We will miss you," Gahdar said after a few moments. The others agreed.

"Don't worry," Sahbaar said confidentially. "We will all see each other again. I don't care what Rahshar says. Someday, we will be together always. Between those times, our friend Akoorah here can fly back and forth with messages and information."

The bird nodded vigorously. "Yes, but you must hurry now!" Akoorah reminded them. "Now is the time to go!" With a few last goodbyes, the lion, rhino, crocodile, and gibbon began to run across the field. The two tigers watched them run up the hill and disappear into the old jungle.

"Do you really think we will all be able to live together again someday?" Bahar asked his nephew.

"I am certain of it," came the confident reply. "I will find a way."

## CHAPTER SIX
## A NEW SURPRISE IN THE JUNGLE

Things in Sahbaar's jungle were back to normal the very next day. It was as if nothing unusual had happened. The remains of Man's wasteful hunt faded away, and soon, the only hint of a reminder was the broken rifles rusting at the bottom of the rock tower.

Every few weeks, Akoorah flew to the old jungle to get a report from Nero and the others. The bird couldn't go any more often than that because the border birds didn't trust her, and sometimes tried to follow her. She had to meet with the friends in secret, hiding in a different unpopulated area each time. The first message Akoorah brought back to Sahbaar and Bahar showed just how suspicious these birds were.

Nero had told Akoorah about a confrontation with them, and she told the two tigers the whole story. "When our friends first returned, they had run to a very dense area Ahgrah knew of. It took the border birds awhile to find them, and when they did, they demanded to know where the four had been all that time," Akoorah began. "The animals had to be clever to avoid lying. 'In the jungle,' Nero had told them. Of course, he did not say which jungle they had been in." Sahbaar smiled when he heard this. "'*Where* in the jungle?' one of the birds had demanded," Akoorah continued. "'All over,' Gahdar had answered quickly. This was also true." Now Bahar chuckled softly. "Then a bird said, 'Well, we have flown all over, and we did not see you!'" Akoorah said excitedly. "'Well, *we* saw *you*!' Ahgrah had fired back." It was Sahbaar's turn to chuckle.

"'Why didn't you call to us?' the lead bird then asked," Akoorah went on. "'We didn't know we were supposed to!' Nero had said in a surprised voice. 'Is this some new law?'" This made the tigers burst into laughter. Akoorah laughed also. "Apparently, by this time, the border birds were so confused they didn't know what else to ask. One got very threatening when he commanded 'Just stay in this jungle. Don't let us catch you outside of it!' Cheerah had quickly added 'We won't!', and Nero said the four had to fight to keep from breaking into laughter."

This made Sahbaar and Bahar laugh their hardest, and Akoorah joined them. Their friends had done a good job of fooling the border birds! The birds sounded like much less of a threat now. The white and brown tiger was hoping this meant he would most likely see his friends again soon. He even wondered if he could somehow go to see them, and perhaps his family.

The more Sahbaar thought about it, the more he wanted to take a turn at sneaking back into the old jungle. He longed to see his parents again. Bahar warned against this, though. He reminded the restless cat that his coloring would make him very noticeable, even if the birds weren't looking directly at him. That gave the special tiger an idea, and he began to search for tasha berry trees. Day after day he searched, covering a huge area of the new jungle. Eventually, he had to admit to himself that for some reason there wasn't a single tree which grew orange berries growing in his new home. This saddened the white and brown tiger.

To cheer him up, Bahar told Sahbaar about a new area of the jungle they could explore. This perked Sahbaar up. It had been a long time since he had done any new exploring, and the thought of it made him feel like a cub again.

The next morning, the pair started off. The new area was a long distance from the lair, so they started very early. Sahbaar would sprint on ahead but was careful not to get too far ahead of his uncle. Bahar surprised his nephew by keeping up quite well, and soon even the younger cat was tired and thirsty.

They stopped at a small pool near the bottom of a steep hill thick with trees and bushes. As they rested and drank, animals native to the area came up and were immediately frightened away. When even the larger predators ran off, Sahbaar was puzzled for a moment. Then he saw his reflection in the water and remembered his different coloring. He had long since become proud of his difference, and he and Bahar had a good laugh about it.

It was very peaceful by that little pool was no other animals around, and the two tigers were just starting to fall asleep when they heard something. It started out quietly, and then began to grow. The sound was similar to Man, but not quite. First the tigers heard one voice, and then a great many more responded. The voices had a soothing and melodic quality, like the birds. This sound was so irresistible that Sahbaar just had to see what it was. The two beasts climbed the hill and peeked through the thick bushes just over the crest.

The scene before them was quite surprising. The fifteen or twenty creatures gathered in the small clearing there looked much like Man the way a panther looks much like a leopard. They stood the same way and had the same type of body, but there were some differences. These creature's hides were a much brighter white than the other Man, and they were covered with brown stripes. While the white areas looked dull and rough, the brown stripes were smooth and shiny.

Sahbaar thought it was quite a coincidence that a type of Man would resemble him so closely. There was one similarity to the other Man that alarmed the tiger, though. It was the sticks that these Man carried. Sahbaar relaxed when he noticed these sticks looked much more like regular tree limbs. The creatures also held them differently, and did not point them or cause them to make any sounds.

"Do you think they are Man?" Sahbaar asked his uncle.
"They do look similar," came the reply, "but these seem much more peaceful." The group had been walking towards the hill when the tigers first saw them, and when they reached a large tree at the base of the hill they stopped. Their singing, which had first attracted the animals, also ceased. The leader made some gestures with his paws, and the whole group set their sticks against the tree and sat down on the ground in a large circle around him next to the tree. They all took something from pouches at their side and began to examine and pick at them while the leader continued speaking softly. Then, one at a time, they step to the center of the circle and placed something on the ground next to the leader. Each one seemed to be adding to whatever it was. As they worked, the chanting began again.

Sahbaar couldn't see what the small objects were, and this was very frustrating. He began to lean further and further out of the bushes, forgetting the fact he was supposed to be hiding. As he stretched his neck as far as he could, he took another step forward. The small rock he stepped on suddenly gave way, and he was so off balance that he tumbled down the hill awkwardly. The tribesman saw him coming and scattered. The cat finally landed with one great thump, flat on his stomach with his legs pointing in all directions. Bahar instinctively started to go after him, but stopped himself and waited in the bushes instead.

Sahbaar raised his head, dazed. The natives had run back just far enough to keep the beast from falling on them, and they all stopped when he landed. The tiger looked around at the group of Man. There was something strange going on. Every one of the tribesmen stared intensely at the animal with the same look of total disbelief. Their jaws dropped as if they were all in shock. The white and brown tiger had never seen that kind of reaction from Man or beast. Then the tribesmen began to move slowly, never taking their eyes off Sahbaar. When they were spread in an arc in front of the beast, they all suddenly dropped to their knees together. Stretching their front legs to the sky, they bowed low enough for their faces to touch the ground. Sahbaar didn't know it, but the natives had seen him before and had been dreaming of such a meeting.

Now Sahbaar was even more confused. What were the silly creatures doing? The tiger just lay there and watched them for a moment. As the crowd continued to bow, the cat looked over to his right. At last, he could see what the natives had been doing. The thing was still too flat to see, so Sahbaar rose slowly and walked over. There, in the smoothed dirt, was a single layer of small stones, all bunched together so they were touching. It took only a moment for him to figure out what the natives were making. Though not nearly finished, Sahbaar could tell the white and brown pebbles were being arranged to create a crude image of a white and brown tiger!

Since the natives appeared to be no threat, Sahbaar turned his head and called Bahar down. His uncle joined him and began to study the unfinished stone picture. "How about that?" Sahbaar said proudly.

Bahar squinted. "Yes, it *does* appear to be you," he replied. "I have certainly never seen any other animal like that."

"Imagine them making a likeness of me!" Sahbaar said in wonder, looking back at the tribesmen. "Do you think the way they are acting now has something to do with that?"

"It's possible. I can't say for sure," Bahar replied. The two tigers went back and lay back down in front of the group, wondering what would happen next. It didn't take long to find out. The leader rose to his feet and said something quickly and sharply. Two natives sprang up and dashed off into the woods. The leader began to chant once again, though much quieter. The rest of the tribe all sat back on their legs and placed their front paws flat on the ground in front of them. Every now and then, they all responded to the leader's chant. All this was very amusing to the two cats, but they also found the rhythmic sounds to be very soothing. They could not wait to see what Man would do next.

The peaceful setting was suddenly shattered by the frantic shouts of the two natives who had left. The leader quickly sent several others after them. The wild noises stopped, and soon the group returned carrying an enormous gazelle. The natives all moved so that the hunters could carry their kill right up to the tigers. Placing the beast in front of Sahbaar, they all returned to their previous positions.

Now Sahbaar was astounded. These creatures were not only apparently in awe of him, but they were willing to hunt for him, too! As Sahbaar looked at the feast before him, the leader silenced the group.

Sahbaar hesitated, and then began to eat. The group first murmured their approval, and then let out a cheer that startled the animal. They all began to chant louder and faster than before. After shaking his head in disbelief, Bahar also began to eat.

As the tigers ate, the leader stopped his chanting just long enough to say something to his people. Several natives from either end of the arc rose slowly and walked back, disappearing into the trees. Moments later they re-appeared, and Sahbaar could see they were leading a huge group of creatures! They were all Man, large and small, but the tiger noticed immediately that all of their hides were completely brown and smooth. The group quietly walked up to the first natives and took their places on the ground behind them in a similar manner.

After a while, Sahbaar and Bahar were full. Since these Man were not doing anything new, the cats rose slowly and climbed up the hill, disappearing into the bushes. As soon as they were out of sight, the natives began to yell and scream wildly with joy, and dance with complete abandon. This sudden explosion of sound startled the special tiger, which had to take one more peek. This frenzied display made Sahbaar more interested in them than ever. He wanted to stay and study these creatures more, but Bahar reminded him that they were waiting to hear the latest report from Akoorah about life in the old jungle. The pair trudged back to the lair slowly, and it was almost dark when they finally reached the cave.

Akoorah had the usual news for Sahbaar about his friends but not much about his parents. Ever since the white and brown tiger had been banished, Gahdar, Ahgrah, Cheerah, and even Nero rarely saw Sahbaar's parents, so news about the tiger's family was scarce. Akoorah didn't want to introduce herself and talk directly to the tiger's parents for fear that even good news about their son would make them depressed about not being able to be with him. Of course, the friends were also not about to tell Sahbaar's parents about seeing the tiger and their adventure. Word of this could find its way back to King Rahshar, and then there would be big trouble. This meant Sahbaar's parents had no idea how he was doing, or that he had met Bahar. Sahbaar thought of this every time Akoorah gave a report, and the isolation made him sad. This time, though, Sahbaar was excited about being able to share his own news. He told the bird all about the strange Man pack they had found, and how they had behaved. Akoorah didn't seem too surprised, especially when Sahbaar was describing their appearance. "You seem to know of these creatures," Bahar observed.

"I have not seen them myself, but I have a cousin who lives in the area where you found these Man. He has told me of a pack of Man with very dark hides like you described, though none have stripes. They have lived in the jungle as hunters for as long as the animals have. There have been many stories of odd behavior by these creatures, but my cousin has never described anything like you have seen. This pack of Man hunts animals for their own food, but they have never hunted *for* animals!"

"That does seem strange," Sahbaar admitted.

"It has to be your difference," the bird commented. "I've thought about this for a while. I now believe it is your difference that saved you when the other hunters were here. They could have easily killed you with their sticks, but instead they went through much trouble to try and capture you alive."

The two tigers thought a moment. "I believe he is right," Bahar said.

"I never thought of it that way," Sahbaar remarked. "It is very interesting how two different packs of Man act so differently. Then there is the third pack that Cheerah knows, that looked like one group but acts like the other." Sahbaar told Bahar and Akoorah the stories Cheerah had told about the pack of Man with pale hides that helped heal the animals. They all agreed Man was a very strange creature. Sahbaar could not stop thinking about the new pack of Man and how they had behaved. He wondered if they would act the same way towards him if he were to confront them again. There was only one way to find out.

The sun was just rising when he and Bahar sent out to find the place again. Akoorah came along so she could see herself how strangely these creatures behaved. Sahbaar was quite excited and kept bounding ahead of Bahar, who had decided to take his time. The white and brown tiger could barely contain himself. Finally, the trio reached the small pool on the opposite side of the hill from where the tribe had been spotted. Sahbaar hardly drank at all, and then turned and started to march up the hill. Bahar and Akoorah were right behind him. When he reached the top, he stopped to look around.

There was no Man anywhere! Sahbaar raised his head high and sniffed. He thought he could just barely detect their scent, which was a bit different from the pale hunters. His nose led him off down the path with the others following closely. Sahbaar quickened his pace as he approached a large cluster of rocks. Already, the others could hear the sounds of Man coming from behind the stones. The white and brown cat stepped right out, expecting the Man before him to begin their bowing and chanting ritual. The natives they encountered *did* act surprised when they first saw the beast, but then reacted much differently. Smaller Man, which the animals determined later were females and cubs, ran to the back of the group as others moved forward. They all began to chatter at once, nothing like the rhythmic sounds Sahbaar was used to coming from this Man. All those in front then formed a wall, and each one raised a long, thin stick. As the tigers stood staring, trying to determine if these were sky sounds sticks or just regular ones, the natives began to throw them. A startled Sahbaar dodged the first few, and then he and Bahar turned and ran. Luckily, the native's aim was terrible, and none of the other spears hit the fleeing animals. As they chased them, the natives yelled "Yi Yi Yi" in a series of high-pitched cries.

Akoorah had anticipated the attack and flew up into a tree. From her safe perch, she could study this group of Man. Sahbaar and Bahar ran back over the hill and to the small pool before they stopped to look back. Man had not followed them. Akoorah caught up and landed on a rock.

"What happened?" Sahbaar said breathlessly. "Yesterday, the pack of Man welcomed us, and fed us, too. What could have made them change their behavior?"

"I think I know why these Man acted this way," Akoorah said. The two cats listened eagerly. "Though I could see the entire group of these creatures from my perch, I did not see any with the white and brown coloring you said those in the group you first met had. I believe this may be a totally different group of Man."

Sahbaar thought a moment. The tiger had been so startled at the pack of Man's behavior that he didn't even have time to really look at any of the natives. A smile slowly crossed his face. "Akoorah, you are right! How very smart of you to notice that!" Akoorah was so proud she shot into the air and flew around the treetops.

"Do you think the first pack of Man is somewhere around here?" Sahbaar asked his uncle.

"Well, we *are* tigers," came the reply. "Let's hunt for them!" The pair set off, this time cautiously creeping through the underbrush and peeking around trees and rocks. They spent all day searching without any luck. Before they knew it, it was dusk. Sahbaar was determined to find 'his' tribe, so he and Bahar decided to stay there for the night. They crawled up onto a rock ledge and fell asleep. Akoorah decided she would rather sleep in her own nest, so she left them there.

The rising sun and their hunger woke them at nearly the same time.

They decided to get some breakfast before continuing to search for the Man pack. It wasn't long before Sahbaar was on the trail of a young gazelle. He crept forward, waited for the right moment, then leaped and began to chase the frightened creature. The animal zigzagged its way around the trees, and then shot through some bushes on its way to a field and good running room. Sahbaar followed it through the bushes, and then stopped quickly when he saw a group of natives a short distance away. At first he was going to run, but then he decided to quickly look and see if any of this Man had the special hides. Suddenly, from the back of the group, the white and brown leader spotted the tiger and began to shout. As he and the other painted natives moved to the front of the group, they all threw their arms up and began to cheer.

Immediately, the leader signaled for some of the other natives to continue chasing the gazelle, which was almost out of sight by now. Sahbaar took this as a confirmation that some special attention was coming, and lay down in the long grass just as Bahar hobbled up. "You found them!" Bahar exclaimed. "What's going on now?"

"Their leader just sent some Man off to hunt the prey I was chasing. I believe they are going to feed us again." Sure enough, to the tigers' delight, the natives returned just then, yelping wildly and dragging the gazelle. Like before, they made their way to the front of the assembled crowd and presented the two tigers with the kill. "You know, I could get used to this" Sahbaar said contentedly as his uncle began to eat. As the pair fed, the natives began to chant softly, their bodies swaying together rhythmically as the white and brown natives formed their half-circle and the other natives filled in behind them as they had done the first time. Sahbaar watched the natives as they watched him. The tiger was still amused at how this group of Man was in such awe of him. Bahar also watched with great curiosity.

Though young, the gazelle was quite large, and both tigers discovered they were very hungry. They forgot about the natives and turned their full attention to eating. Soon, neither could eat another bite and of course became very sleepy. Sahbaar put his head down and went right to sleep, as did Bahar.

A short time later, Sahbaar woke abruptly. For a few moments he wasn't sure where he was, but then he saw the natives still watching him. Something had changed, though. For the first time, there were also young cubs in the pack, as well as females. Like most of the other natives in the tribe, their hides were smooth and completely brown. They had no doubt been brought to see the wondrous sight. Sahbaar nudged his uncle, who sat up quickly. This startled some of the cubs, who leaped back. The leader comforted them, and raising his arm, began to lead the group in chanting once more. This time, something new had been added to the chant. It sounded like "Koo Doo", which the natives began to call out in between their other sounds. At times they would repeat the sound over and over, stretching it out, "Koooo Doooo". Sahbaar decided it was either a new name for him or most likely some kind of respectful title.

It was at that time that Sahbaar felt something on his back. He twisted back and forth but could neither see it nor shake it off. Finally he stood, and clumps of jungle flowers, which had been knotted together, fell off around him. This seemed truly strange, and the white and brown tiger looked at his uncle and saw the same unusual arrangement draped over him. Bahar stood also, and the pair began to shake vigorously to get any bits of flower or leaf out of their fur. As they shook, the natives all threw their arms in the air, jumped up, and began to shout and dance around wildly.

The tigers lay down again, and the natives settled down. They formed the half circle once more, this time a bit farther back. Then, as the soothing chants began, older Man began to bring some of the older male cubs forward. A female brought a large broken gourd to the leader and laid it at his feet. The white and brown tiger could see there was some kind of white liquid in the gourd. As Sahbaar watched with utter delight, the white and brown leader used a broad leaf to scoop up some of the substance and began to rub it on the cub, creating the white around the 'stripes'. The two cats were quite surprised, because they had thought this coloring was natural! Sahbaar watched with fascination as these small creatures became mini versions of himself.

Bahar was getting tired of all the attention. "I'm going back to the lair," he told his nephew. "You can stay if you want."

Sahbaar thought a moment. "No, I'll go back with you. I want Akoorah to go see our friends again." The pair rose slowly and began to walk off. The natives stop dancing and made a waving gesture, calling farewells. As the white and brown tiger walked on, his thoughts were of the two different groups of Man that lived in the jungle, both so similar and different at the same time. Remembering the angry cries of the second group that did not like him, he decided to call his group Koo Doo Man, and the angry tribe Yi Yi Man.

## CHAPTER SEVEN
## CONFESSIONS AND DISCOVERIES

Back in the old jungle, life went on as it always had. The lion, rhino, crocodile, and gibbon continued to play together, though not quite as often. Each had to spend more and more time with their own parents, learning how to find food and survive. Because of this, the time they spent together was very precious. Their favorite spot to meet and be together was at the river. Of course, each time they entered the water and began to splash around, they immediately thought of the friend who they had once thought was afraid of water. Though Akoorah's messages about the tiger helped, it was not like being with their white and brown friend. To comfort each other, they often retold the story of their great adventure, each one excitedly recalling their part in the great plan to defeat Man.

They also talked often of going to see Sahbaar and Bahar again, and even began to make plans on several occasions, but it never came about. There always seemed to be too many things going on, and then there was also Rahshar to think about. The King of the jungle had become much more strict, and even the Jungle Council feared him more than ever. To make things worse, the border birds had talked to the King about the suspicious nature of Sahbaar's friends. They would have to be very careful about what they did or said.

One hot day, Gahdar was soaking in the river. As usual, he lay in the shallow water near the bank with his head hidden in the tall water grasses to keep the river flies away from his face. All that was visible was a large patch of his back, which stuck up above the water. Without warning, there was a sudden, short yell, and something landed square on that patch of the rhino's back. It didn't hurt Gahdar's tough hide, but the animal was startled and stood up quickly. This caused whatever it was to slide off Gahdar's smooth back and land with a splash next to him. Gahdar turned to see a young female tiger cub sputter to the surface.

"I'm - I'm sorry," she said quickly. "I thought you were a large rock!" Gahdar smiled. "That's all right. No harm was done. Say, I've never seen you before."

The cub giggled. "That's because this is only my third time to the river. I'm Alandra."

"Hi, I'm Gahdar," the rhino replied. "Did you come here alone?"

"No, my mother Sahandra brought me here," she replied.

"Sahandra? Why, that's Sahbaar's mother," the rhino remarked. "Hey!

That makes you his little sister!"

The cub's face scrunched up in confusion. "Sahbaar? Who is Sahbaar?"

Gahdar looked surprised. "You mean you've never heard of your older brother?" As soon as the words left his lips he realized that maybe he shouldn't have said anything. He looked down at the puzzled cub, and then felt someone looking at him. He turned to see Sahandra staring angrily.

"Mama, mama, who is Sahbaar?" little Alandra shouted, splashing over to her.

"Alandra, why don't you go play under the trees over there?" her mother suggested.

"But-" Her mother's look stopped the cub from asking any more questions.

When she was a short distance away, the grown tiger looked at the rhino. "We were going to wait awhile before we told her about her brother. We were afraid she was just too young now to understand."

"I am so sorry," Gahdar said in a small voice, his head lowered. "I didn't stop to think that she might not know."

Sahandra's face softened. "Well, I guess you didn't know. It's not like we see you and Nero much anymore since-" She stopped and turned her head as the tears came to her eyes.

Gahdar felt terrible. Not only did he cause problems and confusion for the young Alandra, but now her mother was upset as well, thinking about the son she missed dearly. If only he could do something to make things better. He thought for a moment, and then decided to take a big chance. "Sahandra, if I tell you something, will you promise to keep it a secret?"

The tiger looked at him suspiciously but then nodded her head. Gahdar took a deep breath and blurted, "Nero, Ahgrah, and I sneaked over to the other jungle and saw Sahbaar. Cheerah came over later."

Sahandra was shocked. "Sahbaar? You saw my son? How is he? How is he?!"

Gahdar smiled confidently. "Sahbaar is fine. He has grown up to be a large healthy tiger." Sahandra couldn't believe what she was hearing. She stared off into the distance, thinking about her grown son running across the fields and climbing trees. She was so lost in these thoughts that she almost forgot what else Gahdar had said. "You say you all went into the other jungle? That is forbidden! You could have been caught!" She began to scold the rhino as if she were his mother.

Just then, Nero walked up. He heard what was going on, and couldn't understand why the tiger was talking to his friend this way. Then Sahandra saw him out of the corner of her eye. "Nero!" she snapped, turning to face the startled lion. "You are older, and the King's son. How could you lead a group into breaking one of Rahshar's greatest laws?!"

Nero wasn't quite sure what she was talking about. "Well - I, - um" he stammered. He glared at Gahdar.

"He didn't really lead me," the rhino said quickly, trying to make things right. "We all kind of decided to go help Sahbaar together."

"You told her?!" Nero sputtered. "How could you tell her?! No one was supposed to say anything-"

"Help Sahbaar?" Sahandra broke in. "Help him with what?"

"I accidentally said something to little Alandra. I didn't know they hadn't told her about her big brother," Gahdar told Nero.

"Big brother!" Nero said in surprise. "Sahbaar has a little sister?"

All three animals were talking at the same time now, and no one was able to make much sense of anything. Finally, one voice rose above the others. "Mama! Mama!!" They all stopped talking and looked down to see that Alandra had wandered back over and now stood in the center of the group. "Why is everyone talking so loud?" she asked, looking around, "and tell me about my big brother. Where is he?"

Sahandra looked down at the cub and sighed loudly. "Yes my dear, you have an older brother, and his name is Sahbaar. He had to go away a while ago, before you were born"

"Why, mama?"

"He just did" she replied, trying not to show any tears.

"Oh," the cub said innocently. "Where is he now? Can I go see him?"

"Not now," her mother replied. "Perhaps someday. Now, go play in the water." The cub had many more questions she would have liked to ask, but she knew her mother's tone, and the questions would have to wait. While Alandra was splashing in the water, Sahandra continued scolding the young animals. "I still can't believe you disobeyed Rahshar," she began. "Nero, your own father!"

"Are you saying you think he is right?" the lion said in amazement. Sahandra said nothing. "That's what I thought," he said. "Well, we don't think he's right, either, and even if we hadn't gone over to help Sahbaar, we would have gone sooner or later just to see him."

"Help him?" Sahandra repeated. "You said that before. Help him with what?"

Nero hesitated and looked away. The lion was reluctant to answer because he knew it would fill the tiger mother with fear. Unfortunately, Gahdar did not think of this. "Man was hunting him," the rhino blurted out. "We knew if we didn't help, they would have killed him."

"Man?!" Sahandra cried, more confused than ever. "What is Man? Why was this thing hunting my son?" She was very agitated now.

Nero glared at Gahdar. "I guess we should explain everything now," the rhino said sheepishly.

Nero sighed loudly. "This is going to take a while. Why don't we all relax in the shade?"

They all moved under a large tree and sat down where the tiger could still see her cub. "Now, explain," Sahandra demanded. "Tell me everything!"

Nero began by telling her of the hunters, which many of the animals, like her, had never come in contact with. He described them and their ways in great detail. This made the mother tiger very uneasy. Then he went on to tell her of the first time he had seen Sahbaar standing on the rocks, and how Man's pursuit of him had made the lion feel he had to help somehow. After describing the plan to fool the border birds and cross the field, he told of the many ways they fooled Man, and eventually drove them away.

The whole time Nero spoke, Sahandra had a shocked look on her face. She was relieved to hear Man had been chased off, but still feared for her son's safety. Nero sensed this and tried to think of a way to reassure her. "There's one more thing to tell," he began. "Sahbaar is not living alone. When he first went to the new jungle as a cub, he happened to meet your brother, Bahar."

Sahandra suddenly became very calm. "Bahar? You have seen my brother?" she asked softly, completely stunned once more.

"Yes. When Sahbaar first found him, he was very sick, but now he is fine. He has been like a father to Sahbaar. Your son is big and strong, and also very clever. Bahar is experienced and wise. They are both healthy and very happy. There is nothing to worry about."

Sahandra was once again lost in thought, this time picturing her brother running alongside her son. Then, she became concerned again. "How do you know they are safe now? You said yourself you have not seen them for some time."

"Sahbaar has a bird friend, Akoorah. She flies back and forth between jungles with messages."

"Then I would like to meet her," Sahandra said firmly. Nero and Gahdar agreed, and with Alandra running ahead, all went to look for the bird.

Sahbaar had become very interested in both of the native tribes. He spent his days searching until he found one of the groups. It depended on which group he found as to what would happen next. If he saw white and brown natives in the crowd, that meant it was the friendly tribe, Koo Doo Man, and he would announce himself with a large roar. When he had their attention, he would stroll out of the bushes, lie down, and let himself be pampered. They would always bring him some kind of animal, and while he ate, they would dance, or chant, or perform some other kind of ritual that the lazy cat did not understand but enjoyed watching. On the other days, though, he would find the all-brown members of the unfriendly tribe, Yi Yi Man. Then, the activities would vary, depending on Sahbaar's mood. Sometimes, he would stalk the group until he was nearly on top of them, and then leap out of the bushes, roaring fiercely and pretending to chase them. This would send them all running in terror. They would run into trees or each other and fall down, screaming all the while. This amused the tiger very much. Other times, Sahbaar would wander into the area and wait until the natives saw him and began yelling. Then the chase would be on! Since they always carried their spears, Sahbaar was careful to choose a path through every bush he could find so the warriors weren't able to throw their weapons.

Sometimes Bahar would go with Sahbaar to find Koo Doo Man and marvel over their service to them, but after he made one trip to the other tribe and saw Sahbaar frighten them, he refused to be a part of that activity. He thought it was cruel and disrespectful to another group of animals, and beneath a tiger's dignity. He told Sahbaar this, and at first his young nephew just shrugged it off. It took a while for the message to sink in, and this wasn't really until there was an accident. Sahbaar had jumped out at the group before he realized there were young ones present. In the resulting confusion, several of them were cut by spears, which were dropped or handled carelessly. When the tiger saw the females run to attend to these young victims, he suddenly felt very bad.

The time after that, he found Yi Yi Man, - but decided not to do anything. As he turned to leave, they saw him anyway and began to chase him. Sahbaar had seen the Koo Doo Man earlier, and tried to steer the Yi Yi away from the friendly tribe. He wasn't sure what would happen if they met. Unfortunately, the Koo Doo natives had been moving on their own, and the white and brown fugitive accidentally ran right into them. The result was a mass of confusion.

The Koo Doo natives were quick to react to the charging Yi Yi warriors. They grabbed any kind of stick they could to use as a club. At first, this was to protect themselves, who they thought the warriors were attacking. In turn, the Yi Yi natives, who really only wanted the tiger, mistakenly took this as a challenge. They were too close to Sahbaar's tribe to throw their spears, so they tried to jab their opponents with them instead. The friendly tribe was trying to protect themselves, but then they saw Sahbaar and realized the others were after him, so they managed to form a wall in front of their prized tiger. Sahbaar stood behind them and watched in amazement. Now Man was protecting him from another type of Man! After a short time, the leader of each tribe must have decided to settle things differently. They both began to yell and waved their arms. Slowly, a few at a time, the opponents stopped fighting. When all was quiet, the two leaders began to talk wildly in turn. Members of each tribe began to respond. Sahbaar watched closely and seemed to be able to figure out most of what was being discussed by the gesturing. It was quite obvious that the Yi Yi warriors wanted to get at the tiger. Sahbaar now wished he hadn't teased them so much earlier.

Luckily, the leader of the Koo Doo Man argued just as hard that the animal should be spared. Sahbaar could tell this when they all suddenly began to shout "Koo Doo! Koo Doo!" They continued this chant, dancing around and waving their clubs until the warrior leader raised an arm and said something. Then, a mighty cheer went up among the friendly tribesman. The warriors lowered their spears reluctantly, turned, and walked off as a group. The leader lagged behind, and before he left, he said something else to the friendly chief. Then, he turned to face Sahbaar, leaned forward a bit, and began talking to the tiger in a scolding manner, shaking his finger at the beast as he spoke. Of course, Sahbaar couldn't understand him, but he could guess that the man was telling him to stop scaring his people.

The tiger had learned something. Although the three hunters had also yelled at and been angry with each other, this was the first time the tiger had seen Man actually fight Man. They had even used other objects to fight with, something animals would not think of doing. Sahbaar wondered if the three hunters used their special sticks to fight with each other.

Sahbaar knew he had been the reason that the two groups of Man had fought. He felt bad that he had put the Koo Doo tribesmen in danger. The tiger decided from that point on, he wouldn't tease the warrior tribe anymore. As he watched the friendly tribe began to encircle him, he even felt too embarrassed to let them began their pampering. He turned suddenly and bounded off as the natives stretched out their arms, calling "Koo Doo! Koo Doo!"

Sahbaar went back to the lair and found Bahar sunning himself on a ledge above the cave entrance. Joining him, he stared off into the distance as he thought about the two tribes. "Is anything wrong?" Bahar said, sensing the concern under the concentration. Sahbaar then told him everything that had happened. "I warned you not to tease those Man," the elder replied. "I hope you have learned your lesson."

"Oh, I have," the young tiger replied, "but I hope this doesn't mean there won't be any more free meals," he added slyly, and waited for Bahar to react. When the elder gave him a surprised look, Sahbaar burst out laughing.

Just then, Akoorah flew up. As it turned out, she was returning from meeting Sahbaar's mother and little sister for the first time. Akoorah had spent hours telling Sahandra about her son and brother's daily life. Of course, Sahandra had much to tell her in return. Because of this, the bird was more anxious than ever, which meant she was flying around so fast and in such a crazy manner that she lost several feathers. Sahbaar was very happy to see her and immediately began to tell her of his latest adventures with the natives. Akoorah tried to listen patiently, but she knew her news was far more important. She wanted to be polite, but it was becoming harder and harder to be still. Finally, she exploded. "Sahbaar, I'm sure the rest of your story is interesting, but believe me, you'll want to hear what I have to tell you."

Sahbaar didn't seem to notice the urgency in her voice. "Is it about Gahdar? Did he slip and fall in the mud again?" Sahbaar replied with a smirk, winking at and nudging his uncle.

Akoorah was annoyed that Sahbaar thought her news was so trivial. She had to make him listen. "No, I just met your mother. Nero and the others told her everything," she replied casually.

Sahbaar was shocked. Before he could utter a sound, Akoorah decided to really get the tiger's attention. "That's not all," she added. "You also have a little sister." The two pieces of information hit Sahbaar like a pile of falling rocks. It was obvious which piece of news was more important.

"I have a little sister?" the tiger asked in a daze.

Akoorah smiled. "Yes, and I have met her, too. She is healthy and cute, and full of energy."

"Does she have the same coloring as my parents?" Sahbaar asked timidly.

Akoorah was almost afraid to answer. "Yes, she does. She looks just like your mother." Sahbaar didn't want to hear any more news after that. He just stared blankly ahead. Akoorah sensed this, and excusing herself, flew away. She would give Sahbaar the rest of the news later.

Sahbaar was happy that he had a sister, but at the same time he had to try and not be upset about his coloring. It was proof that the white and brown tiger was truly different. For a short time, he felt more alone and outcast than ever. Bahar and Akoorah tried to cheer him up, but it was no use. Finally, Bahar reminded him of how the friendly native tribe adored him and the tiger felt better, but now his thoughts were of a little sister he had never met. His chances of ever meeting her had recently grown worse. According to Akoorah, King Rahshar had grown even more fearful of those who were different, so he had doubled the number of border birds, to protect his jungle. They now filled the trees all along the field.

Sahbaar began to spend his time in the corner of the cave, not wanting to do anything but lie there. He didn't want to look for either tribe, or even hunt. Bahar knew he had to get his nephew out of the cave and busy doing something. Akoorah was worried, too. Then one day, after much coaxing, Akoorah finally got Sahbaar to agree to climb to the top of the rock tower early in the morning, something that the tiger had not done for some time. As Bahar followed Sahbaar up the trail, he looked questioningly at Akoorah. The bird smiled and winked, then flew on ahead.

The warm sun and fresh breeze felt better than ever. Sahbaar lay down in his favorite spot, stretching out completely along a long, thin slab so that his chin and front paws hung over the front edge of the tower. From there, he could easily see across the field and along the edge of the old jungle. Lying on the ledge had always been one of Sahbaar's favorite things to do. He could stretch out for hours, marveling at how beautiful his world was. Sometimes seeing the old jungle made him wish for his youth, and also made him sad or angry that he would never be allowed back in. Usually, though, seeing it made him even more hopeful and determined to return. His keen eyesight also allowed him to watch the numerous kinds of animals who lived in the field, as they hurried and scurried through their daily lives. It was all so wonderful. But today, as soon as his eyes fell on the old jungle, he became sad once more. Bahar could hear him sigh loudly, and then whimper as if ready to cry.

The old tiger signaled the bird to follow him as he stepped back a bit. "Akoorah," Bahar said in a low voice, "I don't think this is a good idea. How is Sahbaar going to forget about his family when he is staring right at where they live?"

"Just a minute," the bird replied. "We are almost ready." She flew straight up twenty feet and then hovered there as she looked at something in the direction of the old jungle. Bahar stood watching her, and after a few moments, she flew back down. "We are ready now," she announced with a big smile on her face. "Come on. You'll want to see this, too." Bahar followed the bird back to where Sahbaar lay. She landed on a rock next to her friend and then pretended to have difficulty seeing something. "Sahbaar," she said innocently. "What do you think that is over there on top of that rock tower?"

At first, the tiger was not going to get up, but with some nudging from Akoorah, he finally rose to his feet. Squinting in the sun, he strained to focus on the far spot. "What? I don't see anything," the cranky beast grumbled.

"Just wait a minute," Akoorah replied, hovering now. "They were just there."

"They?" Sahbaar remarked. Before he could question this further, he saw an animal climb up onto the flat top of the rock tower from behind. Sahbaar gasped. Even at such a great distance, and after so long, he would recognize his mother anywhere. She didn't see him at first, because she was looking at something down behind her platform. Sahbaar watched eagerly as two small furry paws popped up and slapped the flat rock, and then with much effort, his little sister pulled herself slowly and carefully onto the flat area.

Sahbaar was hypnotized. After shaking herself off, Alandra looked around. Sahbaar's mother saw her son then, and smiled. She lowered her head to the cub, telling her where to look. It wouldn't be hard for Alandra to spot her white and brown brother. To make it even easier, Akoorah encouraged her friend to move over a bit so that he stood in front of a large dark green bush for contrast. Sahbaar stretched his back and legs, trying to make himself as big as possible.

It took a few moments of looking around for the cub to spot Sahbaar. At first she just stared, but then she began jumping up and down in delight, nearly falling off the rock. Her mother stopped her, and the grinning cub sat down so she could wave at her brother. Sahbaar waved back, and suddenly he felt more alive than ever. Then Bahar stood next to him, and they could both see the joy in Sahandra's face. She began talking to her daughter, no doubt telling her about her uncle. Just then, a flock of border birds flew out of a tree. Sahbaar and Bahar instinctively ducked, and when they stood again, the mother tiger and cub were gone. This 'visit' was far too short, but it had still been amazing.

"Akoorah, how can I ever thank you?" Sahbaar said to his friend with tears in his eyes. "What a wonderful thing to do."

Akoorah smiled warmly. "I just thought you should meet your sister somehow." The three began to talk excitedly about Sahandra and Alandra, but their enjoyment was cut short by a strange, yet all too familiar sound. Sahbaar stood, and his head snapped to his right. The others looked also, and a wave of uneasiness swept over them. On the north end of the field, slowly creeping south into the grassy expanse, was the moving Man lair! The clear end of the lair, which Nero had broken with the sky sounds stick, was solid again, and through it, the three friends could see the same three Man hunters

## CHAPTER EIGHT
## THE ENEMY RETURNS

"Oh, no!" Sahbaar wailed. "Man has returned!"

"Man also has a larger lair!" Bahar added. He referred to the trailer that the Land Rover pulled. It was much bigger than the vehicle and was mostly made up of two separate cages. The two tigers and bird watched as the huge objects lumbered across the field.

The leader gripped the wheel tightly, gritting his teeth as they bounced along. He seemed very solemn, unlike the large man and bearded man in the back seat, who seemed happy to be back. "We're gonna get them this time, aren't we, boss?" the large man babbled eagerly. The leader said nothing and kept staring straight ahead. The large man ignored this. "We're gonna get them this time, aren't we?" he repeated to the bearded man.

"You bet!" the other replied. "We're not gonna screw up this time, are we boss?"

The boss began to growl with anger. He spun his head around. "Will you two shut up? Yes, we are going to get them!" he barked. "Stop acting so stupid! You are the ones that keep screwing up!"

"Boss, look out!" the bearded man shouted, and the leader turned his head back and jerked the wheel just in time to swerve around a huge boulder. The turn wasn't sharp enough to save the trailer, though, which was a bit wider than the truck. The corner smashed into the rock, which then scraped down the side as the leader grit his teeth even harder. The bars made a funny noise as they bounced off the rock, one after another.

The large man flew into the bearded man when the turn was made, squishing him against the door. Then the pair bounced back to the center of the seat as the rattling bars vibrated the whole vehicle. When they had passed the rock, the leader slammed on the brakes, which caused the two men to fly forward, hitting the seat and the back of the leaders head. Furious, he threw the truck into 'park' and twisted around to kneel on the seat. "Now look, you two," he shouted, sticking his stubby finger into the men's faces, "this time you two aren't going to act like a couple of trained apes. You're going to do what I say, when I say!" He shook his finger to emphasize each point.

The bearded man looked frightened and timid, but the large man barely noticed. He had been yelled at so often that the words barely had any meaning. As the leader continued to cut the men down, the large man actually began to look out the window. It was at that moment that he looked at the top of the rock tower and could see Sahbaar against the darkening sky. "Boss, look!" he interrupted, thrusting his arm out the window to point. "It's the white and brown devil! Let's go get 'em!" As if obeying his command, the leader suddenly stopped talking, sat back in his seat, shifted the truck, and resumed driving. They had only gone another twenty feet or so when he suddenly turned the wheel to the left, away from Sahbaar. "Boss, you're goin' the wrong way!" the large man said quickly.

"No, we're going the right way," the leader said in a voice that was strangely calm. "We're not going after that tiger. We're going to make him come to us."

"How are we gonna do that, boss?" the bearded man said, right on cue.

"We're going to catch his friend, that rhino, and make the tiger come to save him!" the leader said triumphantly.

"So how do you know his 'friend' lives in the first jungle we were in?" the large man questioned.

"Well, what I didn't tell you before is that when we were in the first jungle, I thought I saw what looked like a rhino. I could only see it from the back and I couldn't get close enough to get a good look at it. Since I know how scarce rhinos are in these parts, I thought it really must have been a water buffalo, or something. There was something else that made me wonder if I was just seeing things." He paused as if he wasn't sure if he should say any more.

"What was it, boss?" the big man asked eagerly.

"Well," the man began slowly, "there was this crocodile right next to the beast, just waiting there. At first I thought the big guy didn't run away from the croc because it was frozen with fear. I was waiting for that croc to take a big old munch out of the other critter's leg, but the croc just stood there. Then it started moving its mouth like it was talking or something! When I rubbed my eyes and looked again, they were gone.

I forgot about it until I saw the two of them together again later. I was going to check it out, but by then we had found the tiger, so I figured I was probably wrong anyhow. Then, when we were in the second jungle by the pit, I saw that rhino and croc standing together and knew they had to be the ones from the first jungle." He waited to hear the men's reactions, then looked in the rear view mirror. Two black faces stared back at him.

"Um, so how do you know his 'friend' lives in the first jungle we were in?" the big man repeated slowly.

The leader just shook his head and let out a long sigh. "I only saw that rhino once in the second jungle. The fact that I saw it more often in the first jungle means it probably lives there. Besides, if I'm wrong, and if that rhino doesn't live in the first jungle, it's not like we can't just turn around and go the other way."

"How do you know the tiger will come to save his buddy?" the bearded man asked.

"Well, he's become pretty bold, as you know," the leader began. Both of the others nodded. "There is a good chance that freak will come over anyway to try and save whatever animals it thinks we are after. I'm sure he'll check up on his buddies, and we'll get him then. If he can't find us, we can always bring the rhino back out into the field. Then he'll see him for sure."

"If we're going to get his attention, let's really get his attention," the large man said. He leaned over the seat and began to beep the horn. Instead of getting angry, the leader helped him hold the horn down as they finish crossing the field.

Up on the tower, Sahbaar could clearly hear the noise. It startled Bahar and Akoorah also. "What new tricks has Man brought with him this time?!" Bahar muttered angrily.

Sahbaar became worried. "I know they saw me. The large one pointed right at me. Yet they are going the other way." He thought a moment, and then his eyes showed fear. "Could they be after the others?"

"It's possible," Bahar replied, "but what can we do about it? There is no way for us to cross the field without being seen. Even though it is getting darker, I don't think it will rain, so we can't use that trick the way the others did."

"It would be harder than ever to sneak across the field with all those extra birds watching," Sahbaar agreed, "but we have to get over somehow!"

"Too bad we can't hide under a bush like Cheerah did," Bahar remarked.

Just then, Akoorah's face lit up. "What?" Sahbaar questioned.

"Well," the bird began slowly. "There may be a way, but it wouldn't be pleasant."

"Tell us, please!" Sahbaar begged. "We must get over to the old jungle right away!"

Akoorah smiled. "Well, all right. Follow me." The two tigers followed the bird to the pond they had gone to before, but the bird led them to the opposite side that was very marshy. "There you go," Akoorah said, landing on the top of a huge weed.

Sahbaar just stared at the thick green muck. After a moment, it hit him. "You are not suggesting, by any chance, that I cover myself with that glop?"

Akoorah nodded, and Sahbaar made a disgusted face. "Well," the bird replied, "You used to cover yourself with sticky berry juice."

"Yes, but this isn't anything like that. It's heavy, and slimy, and --"

"It will get you across the field," the bird interrupted. "This mud is almost the same color as the field grass. If you cover yourself completely and moved slowly across the field, the border birds shouldn't notice you."

Sahbaar sighed loudly. "You are right," he said. "I'm sorry. I thank you for this idea." With that, the mighty beast began to wade slowly into the marsh until only his head stuck out.

"Don't forget your head," the bird called. Sahbaar growled gently, then took a deep breath and went under. After a few moments, he began rising out of the other edge. The green ooze clung to him like a heavy, wet blanket. Slowly he walked out until he stood on the bank, a tiger-shaped green blob. Snorting a few times and gently shaking the mud out of his eyes, he turned and looked at Bahar.

Bahar tried, but could not control himself. He suddenly erupted into laughter so hard that he fell and began rolling from side to side. "Remember, you're next," Sahbaar said loudly. His uncle stopped abruptly and looked at Akoorah.

"You will have to if you want to go along," the bird said. "After all, you will be coming from the 'forbidden jungle'. The border birds wouldn't allow it." It was Bahar's turn to sigh as he stepped forward. Soon, he too was covered. Now Sahbaar laughed at him, though not so wildly.

"Hurry now," Sahbaar said. "We must not waste time." The trio went to the edge of the field. Sahbaar paused for a few moments, then crouched a little and began to creep slowly. Bahar was right behind him. They moved forward a bit and then paused. Akoorah saw some border birds flying towards the tigers, so she flew up to meet them. She was relieved to find they had not noticed her friends, and she steered them away as she continued talking.

The plan worked! Down in the field, the pair of cats moved steadily, choosing a path that took them near as many bushes as possible without straying too far off their straight course. Finally, they were on the other side. When they were safely out of sight of the birds, Akoorah flew down and joined them.

"That worked great!" she beamed. "I almost couldn't find you, just now."

"Yes," Sahbaar agreed with a chuckle. "There was actually very easy, but now I want to get this glop off of me! I'm going to the river."

"You can't wash it off now," Akoorah said quickly. "Someone will see you and report you to Rahshar!"

"I can't worry about that now," the tiger replied. "I needed to conceal myself to get across the field so I had a head start, but now I don't care if someone sees me. Trying to stay hidden will just slow me down, and I have to go help my friends and family. I can't do that with mud dripping in my eyes or making my body stiff. Also, with all the things I have been through, I no longer fear Rahshar! Let him send his guards after me. I will use them in our fight against Man! Besides, I want Man to know it is me they are fighting, and me who will defeat them again!" Bahar agreed gruffly.

Akoorah thought for a moment. "All right, I'll meet you at the river," she said, and flew off quickly. Sahbaar and Bahar moved swiftly now, eager to become themselves once again. Soon they were both in the water, thrashing around so that every bit of the green slime was washed away.

"Ah, this feels much better," Bahar purred.

"Yes," Sahbaar said, looking around. "Say, I wonder where Akoorah is? She's always up to something." Sahbaar began to splash his uncle playfully, then stopped. He suddenly knew why Akoorah had taken so long to arrive. There in the path, the bird hovered above Sahandra. At her feet sat Alandra, her eyes almost as big as her body as she stared at Sahbaar.

They all just stared at each other for a few moments, and then Sahandra spoke. "Sahbaar, can that really be you?" Sahbaar splash to the riverbank, climbed out, and ran to his mother. She cried as the two nuzzled faces and rubbed against each other.

Alandra began to bounce around, shouting, "It's my brother, it's my brother!" Sahbaar licked her face and began to gently wrestle with her, tickling her. She squealed with delight and pounce at her brother.

Sahandra smiled at her children, and then looked up when she heard more splashing. There before her stood her own brother. Bahar quickly hugged her. "Oh, Bahar," she sobbed, the tears running down her face. "I thought that I would never see you again!" He just smiled at her.

"Where is Father?" Sahbaar broke in.

"Your father is off hunting," Sahandra replied. "Since Man has come to our jungle, it is much more dangerous for us, and the food is harder to find. Sometimes he is gone for two or three days, and brings home very little food."

"No doubt because Man has wasted it all!" Sahbaar muttered to himself.

Akoorah was becoming impatient. When she coughed a few times, Sahbaar looked up. "Oh, Akoorah, you are such a wonderful friend. Thank you so much for this." Bahar growled in agreement.

"You are very welcome, but we can't forget our other friends. Remember, they need our help desperately. There will be another time to celebrate family."

"Akoorah is right," Sahbaar said firmly. "In my happiness, I almost forgot why we are here." Sahandra looked puzzled, and Bahar told her of how they had seen the hunters return and knew there were after the others. "Take Alandra back to the lair and keep her there," Sahbaar instructed his mother. "We will be all right." Sahandra was so worried and frightened that she couldn't say a thing. She just turned and hurried off, shooing her daughter in front of her. Alandra didn't want to go, but her mother was firm.

Sahbaar sighed loudly as they disappeared into the brush. "Where do you think we will find the hunters?" Bahar broke in, trying to distract his nephew.

"They shouldn't be hard to find," Sahbaar replied without emotion. "Now that their lair is so huge, there aren't very many trails it will be able to travel down. Besides, you know how slowly it moves."

"Well, all right, then," Bahar replied, becoming serious. "Let's go in this direction, and see if we can find them."

"Good idea," Sahbaar said, turning to focus his attention on their mission. "Let's go. Akoorah, please fly up and help direct us." The bird shot skyward, and the trio was on their way.

The Land Rover rocked and bounced in slow motion as the leader tried to ease the wide load through the tight jungle. The large man and bearded man looked like hula dancers as they slid around on their seat. "Where-are-we-gonna-find-the-rhino?" the large man asked between bounces.

"I've been thinking about that," the leader replied. "That whole pack of animals sure seemed interested in our rifles, and that was quite a plan they cooked up to get rid of them! I figure we just park somewhere in the middle of all this, set up camp, and start blasting. The sound should make 'em come a-runnin'!"

The other two agreed. "It's a calm day," the bearded man said. "Maybe the white tiger will even hear the gunfire from here!"

The leader looked thoughtful. "That could be," he agreed, to the bearded man's surprise. After a short while, they pulled into a small clearing. "This should do," the leader said. He pulled the vehicle forward and into the trees again, so it would be more hidden. This left just the back end of the trailer still inside the clearing. After pitching their tents out of view in front of the truck, they walked to the back of the vehicle. The large man pulled out a rifle, and he pointed it skyward and prepared to shoot.

"Not yet!" the leader snapped, grabbing the barrel. "We have to prepare the trap first." He went to the back of the trailer and opened the cage there. The cage door had a latch on top with a lever that was operated from half-way down one side. The door swung down from the top and had a built-in ramp attached to it. The leader walked into the cage and threaded a green rope through loops in the top of the cage and to the side of the trailer. One end, he tied to the bottom edge of the ramp, and the other end hung free on the side of the cage with a lot of slack in the line so it was not noticeable. Then he left the cage and tied another green rope to the barrel of the rifle. He strung this rope up into the cage and between the bars on the backside.

He told the large man to lay the rifle down, and had both of them cover all the sides of the cage and the ramp with foliage to hide it. Then he had them walk back over to the rifle. "Okay, here's the plan," he began. "You, stand here outside the cage with the rifle," he told the large man, "and you, you stand inside the second cage and hold onto the other end of this rope," he motioned to the bearded man. "No, wait," he thought aloud, then shook his head. "No, I'd better man that role. You would just screw it up." The bearded man looked insulted.

"You stand in the bushes on the side of the cage," the leader redirected the bearded man. "Then Fatty here will start shooting into the air. Don't go nuts!" he scolded. "Just a couple of shots. I'm hoping that rhino is around here somewhere. The gunfire should make him curious. What we want to do is attract him, but not scare him away. When you see him peeking through the bushes, dropped the rifle right there and run away." Both men looked confused as the leader continued. "I'm going to wait 'till that rhino comes out to start sniffin' that gun. Then I'm going to pull on the rope so the gun moves, just a little. Either he'll be scared off, or he'll get more interested. I hope it's the second, because if it is, I'll just keep tuggin' that line until I lead him right up the ramp and into the cage," he said excitedly. "Then you," he added, slapping the bearded man on the shoulder, "yank on that rope, and slam the cage shut behind him."

The two henchmen just stood and stared for a moment, running the plan through their heads. "Great plan!" the bearded man nearly shouted.

"Yeah," the large man added, "but do you think it will really work?"

The leader looked at him in disbelief. "Of course it will!" he cried. "I have no doubt it will work. Now, let's get in position. I want to get that rhino!"

The men all took their places. When they were ready, the large man looked around, then tilted the rifle upwards and fired several shots. As before, birds and monkeys started screaming as the stillness was destroyed, and a shower of leaves rained down on the clearing. The large man paused, looked around a bit, and then started tapping his foot against a rock impatiently. After waiting a bit, he raised his gun and fired again. Then he waited.

Gahdar was on his way to find Nero when he heard the sounds. Since neither he nor the others had seen Man's return he was quite startled, but he knew immediately what the sound was. Like a moth drawn to a flame, he just had to see if it was the same group of Man.

The large man was just about to fire another group of shots when he heard the brush rustle. Then he saw something familiar. As hard as he tried, Gahdar could not peek through the leaves without his horn sticking out. When the large man saw it, he gave a fake yelp of fear and shook his shoulders in an exaggerated jolt of surprise. Dropping the rifle where he stood, he ran off into the bushes. Then he turned around and crouched down, watching to see what was happening.

To Gahdar, these actions made no sense. He knew Man could have easily killed him with his stick, yet he ran off instead. The rhino carefully took a few steps forward, looking around. Then he walked up to the rifle and sniffed at it, then straightened up to look around again. There were no Man around, and Gahdar realized this was a perfect opportunity to take the stick back to the others. Perhaps they could figure out how to use it, and would then be able to chase Man away for good. He bent his head down again and prepared to pick up the stick with his mouth when it moved slightly. This startled him so much that he took a few steps back.

He stood and stared at the object for a few moments before stepping forward again. This time, the stick move before he even opened his mouth. Instead of being startled, he began to get annoyed. Not even stopping to wonder why the stick was moving on its own, he proceeded to step forward and snap at it repeatedly. Each time, the rifle jumped back a foot or so, just out of reach. It was all the large man and bearded man could do to keep from laughing at this comical sight.

Gahdar was so engrossed in his pursuit that he didn't even realize he was walking up the ramp. The leader was growing tired of the slow process, so he gave the rope one last good yank. The rifle leapt from the doorway and across the cage, bouncing off the back bars and falling to the ground. Gahdar didn't hesitate a moment but charged in after it. "Now! Pull the rope!" the leader yelled to the bearded man, who huffed and puffed to close the cage with a clang. The large man ran over from his hiding place, and he and the bearded man quickly pulled all the leafy vines away, exposing the cage.

After reaching between the bars and snatching the rifle, the leader quickly ran around from the back and stood admiring his prize. "I can't believe that actually worked," he said, scratching his head. The two others gave him a strange look.

Gahdar was alarmed. He butted the thin bars, expecting them to snap like bamboo. When he bounced off instead, he became very frightened and looked around for an exit. He butted the bars harder this time, yelping in pain. "What a stupid!" the large man said, and then proceeded to trip over some vines and fall flat on his face. Gahdar began to howl with fear.

"Go ahead, make noise!" the leader laughed. "Make a lot of noise! Get that tiger over here!"

"Ah, boss," the bearded man said calmly, yet concerned. "How are we gonna catch the white tiger when he gets here?"

The leader's jubilation was cut short." Oh, no!" he said with wide eyes, realizing he had forgotten to plan that far. He saw his men waiting for him to answer and didn't want them to know he wasn't prepared. Thinking quickly, he looked serious and replied, "Um -- I mean -- we take the trailer and turned it around. We'll set it up like before. When the tiger comes up to it, he will think the rhino is stuck in the bushes or something. When he goes in to investigate -- wham!"

"Do you think it will really work?" the large man asked once again.

"Of course it will!" the leader said confidently. "I have no doubt it will!" The two men just rolled their eyes. "Come on, let's get going!" the leader urged. "We can back the trailer into that spot over there." The two henchmen scurried off to the truck.

Akoorah was having trouble locating the hunters. Sahbaar decided to send her in one direction while he and Bahar went another way. The two tigers were already heading towards the hunters when the first shots were fired. The white and brown tiger quickly tried to determine exactly where the sounds were coming from. As the path rounded a curve, it came to a fork of several paths. A few seconds later, Nero appeared on one of the paths. "Sahbaar, Bahar, what are you doing here?" he said, quite distressed. "Was that a Man stick I just heard?

"Yes," Sahbaar replied. "We are here because we saw Man returning to the jungle. Bahar and I sneaked over because we were afraid Man has come back to hurt one or more of you. We are searching for Man now."

Just then, the second group of shots were heard. "This way!" Nero called, and led the others down one of the paths. The trio traveled for a while, stopping now and then to listen for more gunshots to lead them. Sahbaar was very anxious, and just as he was starting to get discouraged, he and the others heard Gahdar's cries for help. Sahbaar was about to charge, but then they heard the sound of the Man lair beginning to move. They stopped where they were and waited. Soon the noise stopped, and all was quiet for a few moments. Then Gahdar started to yell again, this time from just on the other side of the bushes in front of the three cats. They all discussed what they should do, and decided to proceed slowly. Sahbaar stepped forward and peeked through the foliage.

The trailer had been turned around. The new cage and open door were covered with vines, and it looked like a strange hole in the bushes. Gahdar's cries came from deep inside that hole. There were no Man around, though Sahbaar could smell them. What he didn't know is that they were all hiding right there in the bushes. This time the leader held the rope to close the cage, and the others stood next to him. The large man kept poking Gahdar with a stick so he would continue to make noise. They watched as Sahbaar cautiously crept out of the bush. He stood in the small clearing and looked around.

"I don't know," the bearded man whispered. "I don't think he is going to go for it."

"Why not?" the leader growled back. "It's not like the rhino is going to tell him it's a trap!"

Of course, that's exactly what happened. As Sahbaar moved slowly towards the ramp, Gahdar finally saw him. "Sahbaar, what are you doing here?" he asked in surprise.

"We saw Man coming," was the reply. "What's wrong, Gahdar? Are you hurt?" The tiger took a few steps closer.

"Sahbaar, stop!" Gahdar called out. "It's a trick! If you come into the bushes, you will be trapped like me!" Sahbaar stopped halfway up the door ramp.

"What's he doing?" the leader hissed. "Why did he stop?"

"I tell ya, boss, I think the rhino warned him!" the bearded man whispered.

The leader jabbed him in the ribs as he replied, "animals can't talk to each other, stupid!" The bearded man clutched his stomach and let out a low moan from the jab. The leader let go of the rope so he could grab the man's head and slap his hand over his mouth. "Quiet, idiot," he hissed.

Sahbaar heard the commotion. He turned to step down the ramp. Seeing his opportunity fading, the leader quickly grabbed the rope. "Grab the rope, you two, and help me pull. Quick!" he shouted. The others did as they were told. Sahbaar froze in fear as what he thought was solid ground suddenly began to rise up. "Keep pulling," the leader shouted from within the bush. The confused animal tried climbing up to the end of the ramp instead of leaping off the side, to freedom. The men continue to strain and groan, trying to lift the heavy cat. As they lifted him higher, Sahbaar began to lose his footing on the smooth ramp. The men all gave one last great tug. With a roar of anger, Sahbaar lost his grip completely and slid down into the cage. The sudden loss of tension caused the gate to fly up and slam with a loud clang. This made the cage vibrate, and all the vines fell off at once like a curtain being dropped.

The men, who had all fallen down like bowling pins when the rope went slack, were covered with vines, which they quickly pulled off. When Sahbaar saw the men, he roared his fiercest, leaping at them. As his face hit the bars and he recoiled in pain, the leader burst into hysterical laughter, followed by his men. "Roar all you want, you furry freak!" the leader shouted at Sahbaar. "I've finally got you now!" As he leaned his face close to the bars, the tiger took a swipe at him, but he pulled away and began to laugh again. This caused the others to laugh also.

"Sahbaar, I'm so sorry," Gahdar said. "If I had warned you sooner-"

"It's all right," Sahbaar replied. "I am not alone." The tiger went to the front of the cage. "Nero, Bahar," he called out, "Go and get Cheerah. Perhaps she can find a way to get us out of these lairs." There was a rustling in the bushes, which the men did not notice.

"We will be back soon," Nero called from within the bush.

Gahdar was frightened. "What if Man knows what you just said?"

"I don't think so," Sahbaar said confidently. "If they had, they would be chasing our friends right now. I guess they don't understand us just as we don't understand them." He tried to comfort the rhino. "While we wait, try to be calm. I don't think Man would have gone to such trouble to catch us if they wanted to harm us now." That was not much comfort to Gahdar, who began to pace around his small area.

The men had heard Nero's last remark to Sahbaar in the form of a low growl. "What was that?!" the bearded man asked, startled.

"Oh, man, do you think it's that lion?" the large man questioned nervously. "Where's a gun? Give me a gun!"

"Calm down, you baby!" the leader barked. "If it had been that lion, he'd be chewing on your face by now!" The large man grabbed his face in horror.

"Just relax, it's O.K.," the bearded man said, comforting him.

The men had settled down and were admiring their prizes. "It sure is pretty," the large man said of Sahbaar, and the other two gave him a strange look.

"Come on, let's get some grub," the leader said. "Trapping rare animals makes me real hungry!" The others agreed, and they all went over to their camp.

## CHAPTER NINE
## A TRAGIC TURN OF EVENTS

At first, Nero and Bahar moved quickly through the trees. Bahar let the lion lead the way, since he had no idea where the gibbon might be. After a while, though, he could tell that Nero was running around in a panic, and not really concentrating. He called for the younger one to stop. "You must think where Cheerah might be," he instructed. "We don't have time to search the whole jungle."

Nero stopped suddenly. "You're right," he said, out of breath. The lion sat down and began to think. A frown crossed his face as he admitted his friend could be in about twenty different places.

"Too bad there isn't some way for us to search faster," Bahar said.
As if on cue, Akoorah flew down to greet the others. "I couldn't find Man," she said breathlessly, "but I did hear their sticks. Oh, hello, Nero. Say, where's Sahbaar?"

"Akoorah, we need to find Cheerah immediately!" Nero said without answering the bird.

"Oh, I just saw her over at the hippo mud hole, teasing the baby hippos," Akoorah replied, somewhat confused. "Shall I bring her to you?"

"Better yet, do you know where the clearing by the monkey vine grove is?" Nero questioned. The bird nodded. "Well, please bring Cheerah there. We will meet you there in the bushes near the great pillar, and please, hurry!" Nero saw the puzzled look on the bird's face and exclaimed, "Man has captured Sahbaar and Gahdar!" Akoorah gasped, and then shot skyward.

On their way back to the cages, Nero and Bahar met Ahgrah. She was very surprised to see Bahar and asked about Sahbaar. Nero quickly told the crocodile how Man had returned to the jungle and had now captured their friends. Ahgrah wanted to help free them, so she joined the others. Soon they were back at the Man lair and crowded behind the bushes. The cages were now parked in the open, with nothing to conceal anyone who tried to get close. Nero called out to his friends. "Sahbaar, Cheerah will be here soon." The tiger looked more relaxed.

The group didn't have to wait long before they heard a rustling in the trees above them. Cheerah slid down a vine and came over to the others. "What is the emergency?" she said, out of breath. "Akoorah didn't say much." She was very surprised to see Bahar. "Bahar! Is Sahbaar here?" she questioned, looking around.

"Yes", Nero replied. He quickly told the gibbon what had happened. "Sahbaar thinks you may be able to free them," he added.

Cheerah pushed through to the front of the bush. "Sahbaar, is it safe to come over?"

"Yes," Sahbaar called back, "if you are quiet. Gahdar can just barely see Man from his side, and he says they have just eaten, and are now all asleep."

The gibbon scrambled across the open area, quickly climbed the side of Sahbaar's cage, and sat on top among the tree branches. She examined the cage. "They have these kinds of lairs at the Man place I visit," she exclaimed. "They are all different sizes, though I don't think any of them move."

"Just try and open it!" the cat said impatiently, pacing in a circle. Cheerah did not know about the lever, so she just tried to lift the latch, but it was heavy, and the weight of the door pulled at it. She almost had it sprung when Gahdar called out, "They are coming!"

It was the leader. He just had to come over and look at his two prizes again. He stood grinning at Sahbaar, who stared back. The tiger was glad he had Man's attention, and he hoped Cheerah wouldn't move. "You thought you were so smart," the leader sneered. He actually thought he had enough control over the wild animal to reach between the bars and touch him. Sahbaar snapped with a growl and tried to swipe at his arm. The leader was too quick, and he pulled his arm away and began to laugh again. He was just about to walk away when Cheerah let out an unexpected sneeze. The leader's head snapped upward and he squinted to look between the leaves. When he saw it was a gibbon, he turned and shouted at the camp. "Quick, you two! Bring the guns! The 'friends' are back again!"

The large man and bearded man had been sleeping quite soundly by the fire. When the leader began shouting, they just lifted their heads and sleepily looked around, but did not move. "I said 'get up', you idiots!!" the leader screamed. In frustration, he picked up a small rock and threw it at Cheerah. The nimble monkey caught the object and immediately threw it back at the unsuspecting man. It hit him in the forehead, where a bump quickly began to rise.

"Oww!" the leader yelped in pain, and he turned to run and get his men up. He started kicking at the still groggy men, which got them on their feet. Like a clown act, the trio then ran into each other as they tried to get to the truck and their weapons. Cheerah quickly began to work on the latch again.

From the bushes, Nero and Bahar decided it was time to act. They guessed Man was going to get their sticks, but the cats thought if they rushed out quickly, they might be able to get to the men first and frighten them off. That would give Cheerah time to free the others. With loud roars, they leaped out and charged at the men.

Unfortunately, the men were too quick. The large man and bearded man spun around with rifles raised and grins on their faces. Nero and Bahar reacted quickly and ran past their foes, disappearing into the brush. The two men were about to follow when the leader called out. "Forget those two! We'll get them later. Help me plug this monkey!" He had already reached the cage, and as he pointed his rifle upward, he began to laugh to himself. In a panic, Cheerah gave the latch one last desperate tug. The latch popped open suddenly, causing the gibbon to fall on her back. The falling door nearly hit the leader, who jumped out of the way. As he began to raise the weapon again, Sahbaar leaped out, being sure to hit the leader in the chest with his shoulder as he leaped. The angry hunter cursed as he flew backward and hit the ground hard.

Meanwhile, Nero and Bahar had circled back through the brush. When he realized Sahbaar was free, Bahar ran out to defend his nephew. The large man and bearded man were ready again, and the bearded man aimed his rifle at Bahar. Just as he was about to shoot, his feet flew out from under him, and the shot ripped through the treetops. Ahgrah swatting tail had done it again! This time the bearded man lay on the ground, face-to-face with Ahgrah.

When the bearded man fell, the large man turned to see what had happened. He grinned evilly as he saw Ahgrah, and raised his rifle to shoot her. Nero had chosen a straighter course back than Bahar. He stood in the bushes right behind the large man, and when the rifle was raised, Nero quickly leaped forward and hit him in the back, knocking the large man flat on his face. Then he scampered off. The large man, certain that the lion was going to maul him, began screaming and thrashing, face down on the ground.

By this time, the leader was again standing. When the bearded man's gun went off, Sahbaar had turned around to see if any of his friends were hurt. That put him directly in front of the leader, only a few feet away. The leader looked at him and snarled. "I don't care about your rare hide anymore," he cursed under his breath. "I'm through with you!" He slowly raised the rifle to take aim.

Cheerah had been watching this whole spectacle from the top of the cage. When she saw the leader below her, she knew she had to act fast. Looking up, she quickly climbed up into the branches of the fruit tree, which hung above the cage. Grabbing the branch above her, she began to jump up and down, stomping on a lower branch. All at once, dozens of pieces of fruit, ripe and rotten, began to hail down on the man. He was hit so hard that he dropped the rifle and fell to his knees.

Ignoring Ahgrah, the bearded man had gotten up after seeing the leader's fate. He was also tired of Sahbaar's tricks, so he prepared to shoot the beast. Desperate and out of fruit, Cheerah climbed higher and could only find a few pieces, which she threw at the man. One rotten piece hit him right in the face, and the juice burned his eyes. He dropped his rifle to rub his eyes as he yelled, then he stepped forward and fell over the large man, who was still lying on the ground, kicking and yelling.

The leader steadied himself and reached down to pull his rifle out from under the mound of broken fruit. Standing, he shook the weapon a few times, and then raised it once more. Pointing it upward, he fired several times into the tree canopy, trying to hit Cheerah. The gibbon screeched and fled through the treetops.

Sahbaar had prepared to flee, but when the leader dropped his gun, the tiger thought about attacking him instead. Before he could act, the man had retrieved his weapon, chased off Cheerah, then had spun around and once again was pointing the special stick at him. Suddenly frozen with fear, Sahbaar closed his eyes and waited.

No one had noticed Ahgrah scurrying around the fallen large man. She had crawled up to the leader just in time, and gave the back of his legs a mighty swat as the rifle went off. The jolt was enough to turn the barrel away from Sahbaar, but to all the animals' horror, the bullet skimmed across Bahar's back and lodged in his shoulder. Bahar roared in pain and tried to run off. Sahbaar followed to help and protect him. Nero leaped between the men and animals. Then, risking his own life, the lion turned and charged at the leader and the bearded man, who were both just getting up again. The large man raised his head, screamed again, and covered his head with his arms. The two others stepped back and fell over Ahgrah, who had stretched herself out. Nero then turned and bounded off to lead the others to safety. Ahgrah quickly crawled off into the bushes.

As quickly as it had started, it was over. Poor Gahdar had witnessed the whole event helplessly and had stomped around in the cage in frustration, butting the bars a few times. When the rifles started going off, the beast collapsed in fright, and now lay quietly whimpering. By now, the leader was so furious he could barely speak. He made a lot of loud angry noises as he got up, and then pointed his rifle in the direction the animals had fled and screeched, "After them!" The bearded man wisely jumped up and began running, but the large man still lay on the ground whimpering, with his arms over his head. The leader kicked him in the side a few times, then just left him and followed the other.

Bahar's fur was beginning to mat down with blood, and Sahbaar was very worried. "We must hide Bahar," he shouted to Nero, "but where can we go?"

"To our cave," Nero called back over his shoulder. "It's just up ahead." It took Sahbaar a minute to realize what his friend was talking about. Much time had passed since the two had played there as cubs, and the tiger could barely remember it. It was a lucky thing Nero had.

The hill Nero and Sahbaar had tumbled and run down as cubs seemed no more than a large mound to the adult tiger. Sahbaar was worried the cave itself would be too small to use. The opening looked barely big enough, and even after Nero dug some dirt out of the way, it was a tight squeeze. Bahar went first, and he roared uncontrollably as his wounded back and shoulder scrapped along the rock. Sahbaar went next, and finally Nero squeezed himself in. As Sahbaar had feared, the ceiling was so low that they had to crouch as they crawled along. Finally, when they were in the center of the cave, they felt they could rest.

The hunters had not been far behind. It was easy for the skilled trackers to find drops or smears of blood on the broad leaves that lined the path. Sahbaar had run closely alongside Bahar so his wounded uncle could lean against him as they moved. This awkward motion had broken many blossoms and shoots, and the hunters were able to spot these also. It wasn't long before the leader was standing on top of the mound. His eyes darted and his head snapped from side to side as he searched for his prey with a crazy look on his face.

Inside the cave, Bahar shifted his weight to get more comfortable in the cramped space, and his wound brushed up against the rock wall. He let out a roar of pain, which the leader heard clearly. The man scampered down to the rocks and eagerly began searching for an opening. When he found it behind the bush, he tried to rip the entire plant out. When this failed, he bent down enough to stick the barrel of his rifle into the hole and began blasting. The first two shots barely whizzed past the animals, who tried to flatten themselves. Nero felt the third split the fluffy end of his tail, nearly nicking the fleshy tip. Worse than that, the bullets all ricocheted wildly off the walls in the dark. Luckily, no one was hit before all the projectiles drove themselves into the dirt floor.

In an effort to see if he had hit anything, and also to get a better aim, the frustrated leader stopped shooting and lay down flat on his stomach, peeking into the hole. When the gunfire stopped, Nero quickly told the others to back into the side niche that the lion had first discovered so long ago. The three adult cats barely squeezed into the space just as the leader began to fire again. The leader couldn't really see, but that didn't stop him from putting six or eight more shots straight into the cave. Because he could now aim, the shots were much straighter, and they flew past the animals, hit the back wall, and came nearly straight back at the hunter. The man scrambled backward in fear as he heard the bullets hit the other side of the rock wall that he lay in front of. As before, the animals were spared by the ricochet as the bullets quickly ended up in the ground.

It was at that moment that the bearded man finally reached the crest of the hill. He had let the leader pass him as he waited for the large man, who was finally with him, puffing hard. The large man had stopped trembling, though he still sobbed a bit between pants.

"Boss, what are you doing? Wait!" The bearded man called to the other. The leader, now a bit dazed, looked up at him.

The large man looked confused. "Why are you lying on the ground? Did you lose something?" he asked in his usual dumb fashion.

The leader grinned oddly. "They're in there," he pointed. "In that cave. I'm going to get them now!" He raised his gun again and peered into the opening.

"Wait!" The bearded man called out again. "We have them cornered! We can still take the white one alive and unmarked!" The leader just looked at him blankly. This made the bearded man pause a moment. The roles had been reversed. He was used to only taking orders from the leader, but now he was in charge. His superior lay on the ground, eagerly waiting for the plan. The bearded man sensed this and confidently continued. "Since they are trapped in that cave, we will just wait 'em out. They have to eat sometime. If we have to, we will take shifts, but that entrance must never be left unguarded. We'll set up a net over the hole, and when one comes out, we'll snare him! If it isn't the white and brown one, we'll just shoot it and try again."

The large man wasn't so sure. "What if he tries to get away?" he asked. "He's pretty strong, and tricky, too."

The bearded man didn't even hesitate. "By then, he'll be so weak he'll be like a kitten. Then we can just wrap a bunch of rope around him," he answered, even more confident. It was a simple plan, but since it meant taking the white and brown tiger alive and unmarked, the leader was all for it. He even volunteered to go back and get the net and rope, which totally surprised the others.

Inside the cave, Nero sighed with relief when the shooting stopped and the men began talking. Cautiously, he peeked around the corner so he could look out of the cave entrance. It was clear, so he edged back out into the middle of the cave to give Bahar more room. The old tiger groaned in pain as the animals all spread out a bit. By coincidence, a few streams of light that filtered through cracks that had formed in the cave ceiling fell right on the trapped beasts in this side niche area. This made the cave seem less dismal. Sahbaar was also able to get a better look at his uncle's wounds.

"Bahar is hurt quite badly," Sahbaar said worriedly. "We must do something!"

"I have been in bad fights with panthers, and I've never seen such a deep scratch," Nero whispered hoarsely, "and there may be a stone from Man's stick in the wound! How can we fix a wound made by Man?"

Nero's words gave Sahbaar an idea. "Man gave Bahar this wound. Perhaps Man can cure it."

"What do you mean?" Bahar asked in a weak, strained voice. "Man does not care about me. They would rather kill me then cure me."

"Not this Man," Sahbaar replied. "The Man Cheerah knows. The good Man. She is always telling us how they care for injured animals of all kinds."

"That's right!" Nero remarked excitedly, "but how are we going to get Bahar to their lair? We don't even know where it is!"

Sahbaar began to wriggle out of the corner. "I'm hoping Cheerah can bring the good Man here, but first I have to find her." Nero and Bahar shifted around so Sahbaar could get out. The tiger crawled to the back of the cave and looked with dismay at the 'secret exit'. The hole, which had seemed quite large long ago, was now much too small for the adult to crawl through. Luckily, the hunters' second round of shots had made many cracks in the stone around the hole. Sahbaar put a paw on either side of the opening and began to push. Finally, after throwing his whole weighed against it, the rocks broke away. "Keep Bahar safe" Sahbaar dared to call out to Nero. "I will be back soon," he added as he crawled out.

It didn't take long for the leader to return with the net and rope. He draped the net loosely over the hole, not even staking any of the corners down. Then, holding the coil of rope in one hand and the end of the rope in the other, he sat down and began to stare at the hole.

The bearded man saw how excited the leader was, and decided to take advantage of this. "Why don't you take the first watch?" he suggested to the leader. "We'll come back and relieve you in a couple of hours." When the leader nodded without taking his eyes off the hole, the bearded man nudged the large man and motion to the camp.

As they trudged off, the large man asked, "When should we come back?"

The bearded man scowled. "Who cares about that?" he snapped. "I'm getting tired of that jerk always bossing us around. I'm getting something to eat, and then I'm taking a nice long nap!" The large man thought a moment, then smiled and agreed.

It had taken some time for Cheerah to calm down. Finally, she made her way carefully back to the Man camp. She had been traveling through the treetops, but when she heard the gunfire of the leader shooting wildly into the cave, she quickly dropped to the ground and hid in a bush, shaking. Gathering her courage, she finally returned to the area. There was no one in the camp except for Gahdar, still cowering in the cage. Cheerah was about to climb the cage and let the rhino out what she heard a noise. It was the two men returning.

As Cheerah peeked from the bushes, the men didn't even look at their captive as they headed for their tent. The bearded man really was ready for a nap, but his anger at the leader had stirred the large man up, and the large man began to complain about his boss endlessly. The bearded man kept telling him to shut up, but it was no use. The pair went into their tent.

Cheerah thought she might try again to rescue her friend, but suddenly the bearded man burst out of the tent with the babbling large man right behind him. The bearded man walked over to Gahdar's cage and sat down on a log, and the other followed, still babbling. Cheerah heard more rustling in the brush and thought it might be the leader returning. Instead, Ahgrah crawled out.

"Cheerah!" she whispered excitedly. "You are all right! Do you know where the others are?"

"I heard many stick sounds from that direction," Cheerah pointed. "I am almost afraid to go there."

"We must!" Ahgrah said firmly. "To help our friends." She looked at the two hunters. The large man had gotten quieter and was just mumbling to himself, and the bearded man was dozing off, leaning against a tree. "These two don't look as if they will harm Gahdar. I think he is safe for now."

"I agree," Cheerah said, grinning confidently. "Let's go!"

The pair set off, guessing from which direction the shots might have come from. Without more shots to guide them, though, they soon started heading in the wrong direction. "Maybe we should each go a different way," the crocodile suggested, not stopping to realize they would not be able to call to each other. Cheerah, who was just as inexperienced at tracking, quickly agreed. They went in opposite directions, each waiting to hear more guiding shots. After a short while, Cheerah heard something in the bushes ahead. She was moving so quickly that she almost ran right into Sahbaar coming through the brush from the other way.

"Cheerah! I'm so glad that I found you!" the cat said quickly. "Bahar is hurt. It is a great Man wound." Cheerah seemed confused. "You know good Man who could cure him," Sahbaar continued urgently. "We must hurry!"

"Where is he?" Cheerah asked. "Can he travel to the good Man lair?"

"No" Sahbaar wailed. "He is in a cave near here with Nero, and he is hurt very badly!"

"Let me see," the gibbon replied. Sahbaar led his friend back to the cave. To get to the back entrance, they had to quietly pass by the front. The leader was still there, in the same position, staring intently at the opening. Sahbaar showed Cheerah the hole in the wall, and the gibbon climbed through. After what seemed like forever, she climbed back out. She was very pale and looked ill herself.

"This is very bad," she said a shaky voice. "I've seen wounds on animals like this at the good Man lair. It takes a long time for those animals to heal, and some don't even survive."

"How far is it to the good Man lair?" Sahbaar asked quickly, ignoring Cheerah's gloomy words. "Will they heal him there?"

Cheerah looked very sad and lowered her head. "I'm afraid he is too weak. The good Man lair is very far from here."

Sahbaar became frantic, pacing back and forth and nearly giving their position away to the leader. "We have to do something," he said desperately. "Can't you bring the healers to us?"

Cheerah thought a moment. "Yes, I think I could do that, but it may take some time, perhaps even a whole day or more."

"We don't have much choice," Sahbaar replied solemnly. "Please go and bring them to us." With that, Cheerah was off. Sahbaar squeezed back into the cave. He crawled over to Nero and Bahar and told them of Cheerah's mission. The old tiger's breathing was heavy and sounded very dry.

"He could use some water," Nero said, reading Sahbaar's mind. Just then the leader, who was still guarding the cave, began to move around. Sahbaar and Nero froze, barely breathing. After a while, Sahbaar heard a familiar sound in the darkness. It was the steady dripping of water. The leader stopped moving, so the white and brown cat decided to take a chance. He crawled forward slowly, letting himself be guided by the sound. At last, the drops splashed on his head. The tiger held his breath. Everything else about the cave seemed the same; could the piece of gourd he and Nero had used to toast their friendship so long ago still be here? Sahbaar began to feel around the area. As if by magic, his paw rested on a rounded object. It was the gourd! Sahbaar pawed at the ceiling a bit until bits of stone broke away and the water began dripping faster. Then he carefully pushed the gourd around in the dark until he could hear the water begin to collect in it.

As the gourd filled with the precious fluid, Sahbaar couldn't help but think back to the day he had first met his uncle. How strange it was to be doing the same thing for him once again. The tiger began to slide the gourd over to the old cat. He froze a moment when the leader moved again, and then pushed the container over to Bahar's head, guided by his breathing. The old one sniffed, and then gratefully lapped up the liquid. It was only a swallow or two, but it helped very much.

"I have to think of something," Sahbaar whispered. "Cheerah is taking too long."

"What else can we do?" Nero whispered back. "Even if we could move Bahar, Man would stop us for sure."

"Who can we get to help us defeat man?" Sahbaar asked.

"No one, I'm afraid," Nero replied solemnly. "Rahshar would never allow it. He would find a way to blame you for everything." Sahbaar knew Nero was right. Still, there had to be an answer. Sahbaar pictured himself and his friend dragging Bahar out of the cave, and Man there, ready to chase him. Then it hit him.

"I know who can help us defeat Man," the tiger whispered confidently.

"Who?" Nero questioned.

"Man," came the reply.

"What do you mean?" Nero said, totally confused.

Sahbaar was already inching his way to the back exit again. "No time to explain," the white tiger whispered back. "You will see." With that, Sahbaar popped through the hole.

# CHAPTER TEN
## A DESPERATE PLAN

By this time, the large man and bearded man had finally come to relieve the leader. "It's about time you two came back!" the leader snapped, jumping to his feet. "What, did you take a vacation or something?" he continued, his voice getting louder and louder. The two men shuddered. Apparently, by leaving the leader to sit still by himself, it had calmed him down enough to where his old personality had come back. "I'm going back to camp," he announced. "I want both of you to stay here 'till I come back -- tomorrow! It will take both of you to watch the opening and keep each other awake." He stomped off through the brush.

"Well, it was fun while it lasted," the bearded man said. He leaned against the rock wall and let himself slide down until he was sitting on the ground. The large man sighed loudly as he nodded, and he sat down on the other side of the opening. Inside the cave, Nero listened to the men, and when they finally sat down and relaxed, the lion sighed, too. He trusted Sahbaar's judgment but wished he knew what the tiger was up to. Whatever it was, he hoped his friend would return soon.

Sahbaar had crept away from the cave by crawling under the bushes. As soon as he felt he was a safe distance away, he leaped out onto the path and began to run faster than he had ever before. He had to get back to his jungle immediately. As the tiger near the field that separated the two jungles, he felt a sudden burst of energy. With a mighty bound, he launched himself out into the wide-open area. The white and brown tiger began to cross the large area with a series of tremendous leaps. It was the first time since he was a cub that he could cross the field with complete abandoned as himself. The feeling was fantastic.

Up in the treetops, the border birds had no problem spotting the mostly - white figure moving across the green field. They got so excited that several of them flew into each other, nearly falling. The leader sent a flock of them to report the violation. Sahbaar knew he would be seen, but nothing mattered now but his plan. He tore into his jungle, shortening his pace but not slowing. There was still a lot to do. At last, he was back at his lair. After pausing a moment to think, he went to the top of the rock tower.

As the cooling breeze blew across him, he finally stopped to rest. He was resting his body, but his mind was still on his mission, and he had climbed the tower so he could search for movement in his jungle. The sun was going down and he was running out of time. It was when he thought he spotted what he was looking for that he went back down to the jungle floor and began his search.

Back at the cave, Nero was getting very worried. Bahar's breathing had become very quiet, and he didn't even moan anymore. Many hours had passed, and the lion had a bad feeling Man was going to try something new. Nero did not fear the two outside the cave now, but he did fear their sticks. That meant the one Nero did fear was off somewhere else doing unknown things, and that gave the lion the worst feeling of all. The lion tried to stay alert, but the stress from their situation had worn him out, and he suddenly fell asleep.

Cheerah had been traveling non - stop since Sahbaar had sent her on her mission. She raced through the treetops, scrambling across limbs and swinging on vines whenever possible. She was moving so quickly and recklessly that she almost fell several times. Much to her surprise she actually made it to the good Man camp by dusk. She was out of breath as she scrambled up to the door, and collapsed in front of one of the doctors.

"Well, hello, Vicky, how are you?" the man said, using his name for her. The gibbon suddenly realized she had to try to figure out a way to communicate her message to Man. As she sat panting and thinking, one of the veterinarians picked her up and carried her inside to a bed. It wasn't until she was sitting on the soft pad that she realized how exhausted she was. She curled up on her side, and though she tried to fight it, fell into a deep sleep.

Sahbaar had been searching well into the night, and had finally found what he was looking for. The Yi Yi natives were sleeping peacefully. Sahbaar wanted to sleep too, but he had to locate the other tribe, the Koo Doo. Luckily, they were only a short distance away. The tiger chose a tall tree halfway between the two groups, and he climbed up to keep watch. Lying along a thick limb, it was only a matter of time before the beast nodded off.

The warm sunlight woke Sahbaar suddenly. For a moment, he forgot where he was, and nearly fell out of the tree. Then he remembered his mission and was shocked to discover that neither tribe was there. He quickly scrambled down the trunk and began to search once more.

Far away at the animal hospital, Cheerah also woke suddenly. The room was empty. She began jumping up and down on the mat, screeching.

"Well, good morning!" one of the doctors said as he entered the room. "Would you like some breakfast?"

Cheerah leaped off the bed and ran right past the surprised man holding the mango. Curious, he followed her outside to see what she was doing. The gibbon had figured out how to tell him what she needed - if she could find it. After searching all the outside pens frantically, she ran into the hospital part of the building, with the doctor in hot pursuit. Finally, she found what she was looking for, a leopard laying on the table with heavy bandages around his leg and waist. In a wastebasket near the animal, the gibbon could see discarded bandages that were soaked with blood. "What is it, girl?" the man asked. "What are you looking for?" Cheerah sensed that she had his attention. First, she pointed at the wounded animal with her right hand, stabbing the air several times. Then, she used her left hand and arm to point towards the jungle. She repeated the action several times, hoping her friend would understand.

The man was confused. "Do you want the leopard to go to the jungle? He can't, he's hurt." Of course, the gibbon couldn't understand him. She kept repeating the actions, hoping it would work. The man shook his head.

Cheerah decided she would just have to take him there. She ran outside and was relieved when he followed her. After running down the path a few yards, she stopped and looked back at him. He just stared back, so she went over, grabbed his hand, and began to pull him along. He finally seemed to understand as he began to walk with her. Pulling him along was going to take forever, though, so she decided to take a chance. The gibbon dropped his hand, scrambled up a tree, and began to travel quickly along the branches. The man made a surprised noise and began to run after her, but then he stopped and quickly turned back, running full speed to the hospital.

Cheerah stopped and waited. She heard a noise that was strangely familiar and was surprised to see a Man lair come down the path and stop. It was smaller than the one the other Man used, and she could see her friend and another inside through the clear part. The other was scanning the treetops, and when he saw the gibbon, he pointed and said something. The lair began to move again towards Cheerah.

Satisfied that these Man were going to be able to keep up with her, Cheerah began once again to move through the treetops as quickly as possible. She soon realized she would not only have to be careful to stay in sight but follow a path that the moving lair would fit down. This became apparent when the lair made a loud noise like the border bird alarm. Cheerah turned to see it was nearly wedged between two trees! The lair backed out and went around, flattening several small trees. The gibbon scouted the area from her high perch and was able to spot a more open route. In an instant, she was off again.

Back at the cave, Nero woke to the sounds of the leader yelling at the two others. Of course, they had both fallen asleep, and the leader was truly furious, shouting that the captives could have escaped. The pair argued back that the net was still in place, and that proved no animal had come out of the cave entrance. Still, the leader carried on. "You worthless slugs!" he screamed. "What if one of them had tried to get away?"

"Well, they didn't!" the bearded man barked back, leaping to his feet. He was getting very tired of the verbal assaults and finally decided to fight back. Thinking quickly, he added, "and even if they tried, they would have gotten all tangled in the net they don't know is here! Then we would have woken up and shot them!!"

The leader was startled but argued back. "The idea was to take them alive. And it was even your idea, stupid!"

The bearded man could not think of a response to that, so he lowered his head and cursed under his breath, kicking at the ground. The large man spoke up to defend his partner. "Well, the point is, they are still in there. I mean, they have to be!"

The leader became suspicious. He snatched the net away from the entrance, pulled his rifle from his shoulder, and quickly dropped to his stomach. He peered into the cave and let out a strangled cry. The sun, which was shining brightly, streamed through the hole in the back of the cave. The leader had not noticed it the day before because the hole was off to the side a bit. It had also been before the gunfire and white tiger had made the hole bigger.

The leader went insane with anger. He leaped to his feet and began cursing profusely. "You idiots! You morons!" he screamed so loud that he almost choked. He started to cough, but continued to yell between coughing bursts. "There's - a huge hole - in the back of - the cave! Thanks - to you - they probably - got away!"

"No, no, no," the bearded man stammered, trying to calm the leader down and shake off the blame. "I'm sure we heard them in there last night making noise."

"You heard them in your sleep?" the boss screamed, his voice getting hoarse. He dropped to his knees in front of the entrance and picked up his rifle. Jamming the barrel into the hole at an angle, he fired several shots that zoomed around the cave. Nero let out a huge roar in fright, but also in frustration and anger. This was enough to satisfy the leader. "You're lucky," he said calmly, getting to his feet and replacing the net.

"So, should we get another net for the back?" the large man asked, trying to calm the leader as he scrambled to his feet.

The leader calmed down and thought for a moment. "No, I've got a better idea!" he replied, smiling slyly. "As long as we have another opening, we'll build a fire in front of it and fan the smoke inside. That should speed things up!"

"Yeah, yeah!" the large man cheered, bouncing around like a child and clapping. "Smoke them out! Smoke them out!" The bearded man thought it was a good idea, though he wouldn't admit it. Without saying a word, he began to help the large man collect wood. Satisfied, the leader picked up his rifle and began to look for a way to the other side of the cave.

Inside the cave, Nero was worried about all the yelling and movement. He looked at Bahar, who seemed to be sleeping peacefully despite all the noise. Then the lion turned his head towards the back of the cave and wished that the white and brown tiger would poke his head through the opening. *Sahbaar, where are you?* he thought desperately. Sahbaar was far away, still looking for the natives. There was someone much closer to Nero and Bahar who would be able to help, though.

It was Ahgrah. Since she and Cheerah had taken separate routes while trying to find the others, the poor crocodile had been searching for her friends almost non-stop. She had barely paused to eat or sleep and had become very discouraged when she finally heard the leader's morning round of gunfire. Luckily, all this time Ahgrah had been traveling in great circles and was quite close to the cave. She quickly made her way through the brush and was finally able to hear Man's voices. Ahgrah slowly pushed her nose between two small bushes until she could see the scene at the front of the cave. Seeing the net, she figured out that one or more of her friends must be inside. The crocodile was then surprised when all three men walked away from the cave entrance at once. She was tempted to scurry up to the hole, pull the net away, and call into the opening. Before she could act, the leader returned. The crocodile then heard noises in the bushes and decided to see what the two others were doing.

The leader had suddenly realized he had left his post unguarded. He waved his hand in the general direction his men should go. "I'm sure there's a path through there," he growled. "Use your brains for once!" he added before hurrying back to the front cave opening. Ahgrah quietly followed the others as they found their way to the back and then dropped their wood next to a sloping slab of rock that had a jagged hole in it. Ahgrah couldn't understand the purpose of this but had a strange feeling it was not good. After the men had piled up all of their sticks directly beneath the hole, the bearded man pulled something out of his pocket, knelt down, and waved it beneath some sticks. Ahgrah was shocked when she saw the flames appear and spread quickly. The extra dry wood was burning fast and not producing much smoke, so the two men headed into the bushes to search for greener sticks.

Ahgrah watched as a thin stream of smoke floated up and seemed to be sucked into the hole. When she faintly heard Nero cough a few times, she suddenly realized what Man was trying to do. Almost without thinking, she ran up to the fire, positioned herself, and began slapping at the pile of wood with her tail. Of course, she had no idea the flames would be so hot, but she grit her teeth and kept swatting until the fire was destroyed. Then she quickly scurried back under the bushes and turned to watch.

The two men came running back to see what all the commotion was. They stared in disbelief at the mess, but then the bearded man calmly began to rebuild the fire, adding the new pieces. Once the wood was blazing again, he told the large man to help him search for more sticks. This time, though, the bearded man stopped his partner on the other side of the bushes and motioned him to turn and help watch. As before, Ahgrah quickly scurried out and began to swat at the fire. The bearded man leaped out from his hiding place with a loud "aha!" and pulled a pistol from his belt. He quickly began to fire at Ahgrah. She was terrified, but the brave animal held her ground long enough to destroy the fire again before fleeing. The angered man had only managed to squeeze off two or three shots, and they had all missed.

The bearded man cursed as he reloaded the gun. "Pile this wood up and start the fire again," he called to the large man, tossing him his lighter. "I'm goin' on a croc' hunt!"

Sahbaar had been searching for the natives for almost a half day, had found them, then lost them again as he slept. Now, nearly another half day of non - stop searching had gone by, and the tiger was nearly beaten. He was about to go back to the rock tower and try to see something from there again when he heard familiar sounds. Barely pulling himself up a large tree, he looked around. Tears of relief came to his eyes when he saw the Koo Doo tribe only a short distance away. He quickly began to climb down to search for the Yi Yi warriors. Forgetting how weak he was, he leaped onto a lower branch, and the force of landing there made his legs crumble. He nearly fell onto some rocks but managed to grab the limb and hang on. The exhausted tiger crawled down the rest of the way very slowly.

After looking for the Yi Yi for just a few minutes, he stopped at the base of another large tree and looked up slowly, not wishing to have to climb again. Just then, he heard a soft noise growing louder. Sahbaar sat and rested for a few minutes, letting the familiar noise come to him. When the chatter seemed to stop moving, he stepped forward and stuck his head through the bushes. He sighed loudly with relief as he saw the members of the Yi Yi tribe taking a rest.

The white and brown tiger sat down again. All his muscles were sore, and he was so weak he could barely sit up, yet he had to keep going with his plan to make the tribesmen chase him. For a moment, he wondered what would happen if the Yi Yi warriors were to actually catch him, a real possibility in his current state. They would surely not spare him, and the Koo Doo tribesman might not even be able to save him. All that faded away, though, when he thought of his uncle. Not only could it be too late for him, but also for the first time Sahbaar realized how much danger Nero was in. The tiger could lose his best friend forever.

All at once, a strange feeling came over the white and brown tiger. It was as if someone was pouring pure energy into the animal's body. His lungs filled more deeply, his heart beat stronger, and it was like the aching muscles had been replaced with fresh young ones. Standing confidently and taking a few deep breaths, he leaped through the bushes and into the center of the Yi Yi tribesman. For a moment, everyone froze. The natives were all surprised to see their foe again but quickly reacted. A deafening cry went up from the group as they grabbed spears, tree branches, and even plant stalks, roots and all. They began to come at the tiger, and he nimbly turned and dashed off the way he came. As the natives began to throw the items, Sahbaar ducked and began running under and through bushes just like old times. Luckily, the natives aim hadn't gotten any better, and none of their weapons even came close to striking the hero.

Sahbaar did not play this time but took the straightest course back to the Koo Doo tribe. The tiger wished his greatest wish that they would still be where he had seen them last. When they were not, he panicked for a moment, but then heard them further up ahead. As he reached them, he was sure to leap into the air so that they could clearly see it was him being chased again. Many of the Yi Yi natives, blinded with rage, knocked down the Koo Doo natives as they ran into them. Sahbaar had hoped this would happen, as they would make all the Koo Doo angrier and ready to fight. When he felt the entire group was behind him, he turned the swarm back towards the old jungle.

The border birds were just beginning to doze on their branches when the white and brown tiger and his swarm of natives exploded from the banishment jungle and into the field. Birds flew into each other as the whole flock rose together. When they had reported earlier that Sahbaar was seen returning to the banishment jungle, the King was outraged. He roared at them for not seeing the white and brown tiger leaving his jungle in the first place. Rahshar threatened that if they made the same mistake again, their punishment would be severe. Now was their chance to redeem themselves, and perhaps the tiger would be caught and be dealt with. This time, the entire flock raced to tell the King.

The bearded man had been searching for Ahgrah, who was very good at hiding under low, dense bushes. She even snuck up on him a few times and knocked him down with her tail, trying to get him to drop his short stick. Unfortunately, the bearded man hung on tightly to the weapon. Each time he fell, he jumped up, cursing more and more until he was blinded by rage.

The leader had been waiting for huge clouds of smoke to billow out of the entrance. When only a few wisps wafted out, he stomped to the back of the cave to see what was taking so long. When he saw the large man trying to start the fire again, he exploded. "What's wrong with you?" he shouted, kicking at the cowering man who squatted next to the wood. "Don't you have that thing going yet? My dog can build a better fire, and faster, too!" He looked around. "Who was shooting? Where's your equally helpless partner?"

"He's out there hunting that stupid croc," the large man snarled, pointing a stubby finger. "It's not our fault the fire isn't going! That crocodile kept putting it out! He won't anymore, though!"

The leader shook his head angrily and threw down his rifle. He pulled the sticks from the large man's hands and plopped them on the pile. "Light that," he barked, then picked up his rifle and began to go after the bearded man. A short distance away, Ahgrah's keen hearing picked up the crackling of the fire, and she could see the flames clearly from under the bushes. Quickly, she began to scramble towards the light. The bearded man saw the movement and began to chase her. Just then the leader stepped into the path ahead, and without slowing down, Ahgrah scurried right between his legs and kept going. He turned his head to watch her in disbelief. The bearded man, flailing his arms to push the bushes out of the way, ran into the leader so hard that the pair flew five feet before hitting the ground with a solid thud. Their rifle and pistol were launched deep into the surrounding foliage, and they both lay moaning.

Ahgrah ran right up to the large man, opened her mouth all the way, and let out a crocodile roar. The large man screamed and ran off into the bushes. Ahgrah positioned herself triumphantly and began to swat away the logs, making sure the fire was completely out once more.

The leader and the bearded man got up slowly. The leader was about to yell at the other, but when he saw the fury in the bearded man's eye he decided not to provoke him anymore. Turning back to go to the fire, he stopped abruptly as he could just barely hear a faint rumbling sound. At first, the leader thought it might be thunder in the distance, but as the sound grew louder, it was joined by a strong high-pitched cry, as if made by dozens of creatures.

Confused, the leader stopped the bearded man so he could listen also. They finally determined the direction the sound was coming from. "Get up this tree, and find out what that blasted noise is," the leader snapped, shoving the bearded man against the trunk. The bearded man sighed and began to climb. When he found a good limb to stand on, he shaded his eyes and squinted. It was hard to know exactly where to look. Finally, he spotted something. A wide patch of vines and tall weeds were being pushed aside or flattened in a line heading straight towards the two men.

"Something big is coming," the man in the tree called to his boss, "and it's coming fast!" He suddenly lost his footing, grabbing the trunk, and slid painfully down the tree, landing on his boss. They scrambled to their feet quickly. Fearing an elephant stampede, they began running back towards camp. Up the trail a bit, they met the large man. As they ran past, he shrugged his shoulders and started running after them. At one point, the leader looked over his shoulder and realized it was a swarm of running natives who were causing the commotion. He scrambled up onto a huge rock slab that jutted out of the ground about four feet. His men joined him, and the hunter caught his breath and tried to see what was going on. Sahbaar, who was well ahead of the natives, was delighted when he looked on ahead and saw the three hunters climb onto the rock. This meant he must be close to the cave. He began to leap as he ran so the leader could clearly see him. The man was surprised and angered to see the tiger out of the cave. He reached for his pistol, and then remembered he had left it back at camp. Furious and totally frustrated, he bent over to scoop up an armful of small stones. He began to throw them at the cat, trying to hit him in the face. His anger made his aim so bad that the stones flew past and began hitting the natives.

The Koo Doos had caught up to and mixed in with the Yi Yi natives by this time. As members of both tribes were being pelted, they forgot about their original conflict and turned their attention towards these pale Man. Swarming around the rock, they began to reach for the trio, shouting in anger. The leader didn't realize he had hit any of the natives, and couldn't understand why they were so upset. This new distraction just annoyed him at first, but he became fearful when the crowd pressed in harder. Still, they were not going to keep him from his prize, and he picked up a fallen tree branch leaning against his perch and began to swing it at the natives as he looked for Sahbaar.

When the natives circled the men, Sahbaar dived into a thick bush and hid there. With the first few swings of the branch, the leader had caught the closest natives off guard and had knocked many down. This made the remaining members of both tribes furious, and they shouted louder as they tried to climb onto the rock. The leader then noticed that the large man had a pistol tucked in his belt. He pulled it out and pointed it at the natives. They knew what it was but immediately started grabbing at it anyway. The leader was about to pull the trigger when a native almost pulled the gun out of his hand. The poachers were beginning to feel trapped. Fighting the natives off, the leader and his men leaped off the backside of the rock and began to run. All the natives began to climb over and around the rock in hot pursuit, yelling all the while.

All this time, Cheerah had desperately been trying to guide her Man friends and their lair back to her animal friends. After taking several turns that they could not fit through, the gibbon finally found the road the hunters had made. Hopping down onto the hood of the hospital jeep, she jumped up and down, pointing urgently as the men continued to drive. Finally, they came upon the poacher's camp.

The doctor driving the jeep stopped and got out. The other man, who was a game warden, followed him. "What in the world-" was all the doctor could say as he looked around at the vehicles. Cheerah immediately scrambled over to the cage where poor Gahdar had been locked all this time. The gibbon began to screech so her friends would notice the cage, and then quickly climbed up to open it.

"Oh, Cheerah," Gahdar wailed. "I am so happy to see you! I have heard many stick sounds and other noises in the distance, and I feared the worst!" Cheerah tried to soothe her friend, telling him help had arrived as she pulled at the latch.

The huge gate on the cage had barely clanged open when everyone heard a chorus of loud sounds. It was the screams of the hunters as they headed for their truck and the shouts of the natives chasing them. Gahdar trotted down the door ramp of the cage just as the three hunters came into view down the trail. The rhino snorted and began to charge. The leader screamed louder than the others as he frantically looked for another route. Not thinking clearly, he spotted a large old tree nearby that had been pushed over to a sharp angle by a storm. Without slowing his pace, the leader ran right up the topside of the trunk until he slipped, grabbing branches. He continued to climb quickly, with the two others right behind. Surprisingly, the large man made his way up past the others; then the bearded man pushed the leader out of the way to get to a safer spot. A few natives began to climb up after them, but when the leader pointed his pistol at them, they backed down.

The trio climbed as far as they could, hopelessly trapped fifteen feet off the ground. The leader kept everyone else away by waving his gun around the crowd. This standoff lasted for several minutes before Cheerah's Man friends ran up, with Cheerah and Gahdar right behind. The taller man fired his own pistol into the air. This silenced the crowd. "What is going on here?!" Cheerah's doctor friend demanded angrily. "Who are you three?"

The large man and bearded man looked around innocently, and the leader glared at them and growled, "Keep quiet!" While the game warden and the doctor waited for their answer, Sahbaar quietly came up behind the group. He sighed with relief when he saw that not only had the natives treed the bad Man away from the cave, but Cheerah's help had arrived also. This relaxed him greatly, so he was totally unprepared for what he saw out of the corner of his eye. A little bush rustled gently, and out popped a small tiger cub that looked around casually. Sahbaar blinked twice. It was Alandra!

As the white tiger watched in fear, his little sister began to walk over to where Cheerah stood. "Cheerah," she called out, "have you seen my brother?" Almost certain something would happen to her, Sahbaar raced towards her. The leader saw this and quickly aimed his pistol and fired at his enemy. He was so aggravated that the shot didn't even come close, and Sahbaar nimbly grabbed his sister by the nape of the neck and disappeared into the brush.

The leader prepared to fire again, but a Koo Doo native who was holding a rock threw it and knocked the pistol out of his hand. The leader yelped in pain but quickly twisted his body so he could try to pull a knife from the bearded man's belt. He had barely touched the weapon when Cheerah's taller friend called, "Hold it right there!" over the noise of the grumbling natives. The leader turned to see the game warden, who was now holding his pistol on them. The leader raised his hands, as did his men. Cheerah and Gahdar were relieved to see Man was now pointing a sky sound stick at Man rather than them! When the natives saw the pistol fall, they all tried to climb the tree to get at their non-threatening enemies. Still confused, the doctor yelled something and suddenly all the natives stopped yelling and reaching for the hunters.

Now that things had settled down, the doctor had a chance to look around. "Look at this!" he said to the warden as he admired Gahdar. "A full-grown rhino just standing here! It's almost as if it was tame!" Poor Gahdar was not tame; he was just too exhausted from all that had happened to move. The doctor began to pat and stroke the rhino as he checked him, though, and soon the beast felt much more relaxed.

"That's not all," the game warden replied, never taking his eyes off the trio. "I swear that thing that ran off just now was a white and brown tiger!"

"That would explain the natives with the stripes being here," the doctor replied. "The fact that they have painted themselves means that they have actually found one!"

The game warden was surprised. "You mean there really is a white tiger with brown stripes running around here somewhere? I thought those things were just a local myth."

The doctor shook his head. "No, there really was one here long ago. The doctors who started the animal clinic I run saw it with their own eyes, and even took pictures. This tribe found it, and it became the center of their whole culture." The man then looked up at the poachers. "I'll bet that's what these three were after. It would have made quite a prize. Luckily, we got here in time to stop that."

"Right. Back to business," the warden replied. He looked back at the three hunters in the tree. "All right, you three, start talking. We've seen the cages, so it might as well be the truth," he added.

The large man sighed loudly. "You'd better keep your large, stupid mouth shut!" the leader growled. That was the last straw! The large man snapped, and he reached around the bearded man and hit the leader in the back of the head with his closed fist. The startled hunter couldn't grab a branch in time and fell, and the agile natives below him jumped out of the way so he hit the ground flat on his back. As he lay groaning, the other two in the tree began chattering all about the things they had done as instructed by their boss.

In all the excitement, Cheerah had almost forgotten about the others. Now that the three men were no longer a threat, the gibbon grabbed the doctor's hand and pulled him down the trail to the cave. Gahdar followed them and yanked the net out of the way with a flip of his horn. Cheerah stuck her head into the cave. "Nero! Is Bahar still all right?" she called to her friend.

"Cheerah," came Nero's shaky voice back through the darkness. "At last you are here! What is happening?"

"The evil hunting Man have been captured and are no longer a threat. I have one of my Man healer friends here with me. Is Bahar all right?" she repeated.

"Bahar is barely breathing, and I fear he is too weak to move."

"Come out, and let my Man friend in," the gibbon replied. The doctor was startled when the weak, coughing lion dragged himself out of the small hole, but the man did not hesitate when Cheerah pulled him forward and motioned for him to enter. The doctor produced a flashlight, and the animals marveled at this new stick that brought the sun into the cave. He found Bahar, and with one glance, the doctor knew the severity of the wound. He used all his strength to pull the tiger out of the cave by his front paws.

Bahar was limp and unconscious. It was too far to drag him back to the jeep. "Gahdar," Cheerah suggested. "Can you get down far enough so my friend can pull Bahar onto your back?" Again, the doctor was amazed as the rhino lay down on his stomach, and the gibbon showed the man how to pull the wounded tiger on. Just then Ahgrah came out of the bushes, covered with burns. She limped slowly, and Cheerah motioned for her to follow the procession.

Sahbaar had carried his sister far from the others before setting her down. He had just begun to scold her when Sahandra came through the bushes. Her terrified look changed to joy when she saw her son was safe. Sahbaar could only let himself give his sister and mother a quick hug before finding out what had happened to his friends. He sent the two females off, and he crept back to the clearing and peeked through the bushes.

Cheerah and her doctor Man friend were gone. The tall Man had a short sky sound stick pointed at the two Man in the tree. Sahbaar's heart began to pound until he saw the leader on the ground, just beginning to sit up. The Man with the sky sound stick said something that all the natives understood. They moved away so the large man and bearded man could come down. They helped the leader up, who began to fight them. Then the one good Man said something to the three of them, and they stretched their front legs up and began to walk back to their own cages. Sahbaar grinned as the Man with the sky sound stick put the two Man in one cage, and the angry Man in the other.

Then, Sahbaar turned to see Cheerah and her Man friend coming down the path. Gahdar was next with Bahar across his back, and then Ahgrah. Gahdar followed the Man to his small lair, where the doctor gently slid Bahar onto a flat plank in the back. Then the doctor finally noticed the blistering burns on Ahgrah's snout, lower back, and tail. "What did they do to you?" he mumbled as he gently tried to examine the wounds.

Cheerah watched this and knew he wanted to help her. "Go with Man," she instructed her friend. "He will help you, too." The gibbon pulled another backboard out of the jeep and made a ramp for the crocodile to crawl up.

The doctor watched in awe as the creature climbed up the board without any coaxing. "Thanks, girl," he said to Cheerah as he closed the back gate.

As the jeep started up, Cheerah quickly went over by Sahbaar, who had called to her. "Bahar and Ahgrah are going to be fine, I know it," Cheerah reassured her friend confidently. "I trust these Man, and I will visit them often until our friends are both well." The gibbon scampered back to the small lair, hopped in, and the doctor drove away. At the same time, the other man drove off in the large lair, with the leader still trying to grab the other two through the bars.

At last, Sahbaar thought he could rest. Nero, who had stayed out of the way when Bahar was being attended to now joined Sahbaar and Gahdar. Since the lion could only hear and imagine what had gone on from inside the cave, he was curious to know what had really happened. The two others told him everything they had witnessed. Since the good Man had taken the bad Man away in their own cages, Sahbaar was certain that this time the hunters would not return. The three friends were overjoyed that it was all finally over. Of course, that was not meant to be, just yet. Akoorah flew up just then, breathlessly warning Sahbaar that Rahshar knew he had returned, and the tiger was to turn himself in and face his punishment. Sahbaar thought for a moment. "Tell him I will soon, but not right now." Sahbaar wanted to wait for his friend Ahgrah and uncle Bahar to come back to the jungle. Only then, before them and all the creatures of the jungle, would he face King Rahshar and demanded his acceptance.

## CHAPTER ELEVEN
## THE FINAL SHOWDOWN

    Sahbaar knew it would take some time for his uncle and friend to heal, and after being with his sister and mother again, the tiger could not bear to go back to the banishment jungle to wait. He also desperately wanted to see his father. It was Akoorah who suggested that Sahbaar stay in the secret cave, which was still unknown to the other animals. So Sahbaar stayed there and waited, hunting at night and staying inside during the day. His friends visited him often inside the cave, where they talked about all of their adventures. Gahdar was much too big to fit in the cave, but he lay near the entrance, now hidden by a huge mound of vines, where he could hear everything and also talk to the others. Nero even brought Sahbaar's family to the cave under the cover of darkness to see Sahbaar. Outside of the cave, Alandra would ask when he could come home to be with the family, and Sahbaar would smile and say, "Soon". Sahandra was worried about Rahshar's threats, but Sahbaar promised her he would deal with that problem successfully in time.

    Besides visiting with the white tiger, Sahbaar's friends had a new game. They discovered Rahshar had been receiving daily reports from the border birds that confirmed that the white tiger had not returned to his jungle. The King was determined to find this offender, so he sent out a huge group of monkeys to search for Sahbaar. Some would follow Nero, Gahdar, Cheerah, and even Akoorah, waiting for them to give up Sahbaar's hiding place. Others spent hours searching every bit of the jungle. Since the monkeys were so noisy and clumsy, they weren't any good at following their subjects without being noticed, and they kept forgetting where they had already searched. Because of this, Sahbaar's friends had great fun leading these 'spies' in circles and luring the searchers away from the cave. Sahbaar's family even joined the fun when some monkeys began to follow them.

    The tiger's friends did more than play, though. When Man had finally been caught and Bahar and Ahgrah saved, there had been other animals that had witnessed this. Stories quickly began to spread about the banished tiger that had saved the day, and the others who had chosen to ignore his difference and risked their own lives to help him. Some animals began to wonder if Sahbaar was really such a threat after all. Whenever one of the tiger's friends happened upon a group discussing this, they quickly did all they could to convince the others that Sahbaar was as good and noble as any other animal.

Soon, animals began to seek out Sahbaar's friends and asked them to tell of their adventures with the white and brown tiger and Man. What had started as a few animals talking quietly here and there about the things that had happened turned into daily chatter about whether or not the tiger's banishment had been fair. Word of this quickly got back to Rahshar. He began to worry that all the residents of the jungle would rise up against him. The King was certain Sahbaar's friends knew where the white tiger was hiding, so he decided to pressure them directly. He sent the largest bears out to find Nero, Cheerah, Gahdar, and Akoorah, and bring them to him.

The four friends all happened to be outside the secret cave when the bears found them, and the large beasts grabbed them immediately. They put up a fight, but Sahbaar called out from inside the cave, "Don't fight them or they will hurt you!"

"Who said that?" one bear growled.

"Me," Nero said quickly. "We will go with you."

Nero had not lived at his family's lair for some time, and it felt strange to be back there under these circumstances. Rahshar was pacing impatiently. "I will make this brief," he began. "Bring Sahbaar to me tomorrow morning, or else."

"Or else what?" Gahdar snapped, daring to challenge the King. All the recent adventures had made the rhino very brave.

"Let's just say it will be a state far worse than banishment!" the King said with a mighty growl in his voice. Nero was shocked at how his own father could threaten his friends, and Rahshar could tell this by the look on his son's face. "You have not been a very good example to the others," he said to Nero, who just stared back at his father. "I expect Sahbaar to meet me in the field by the bamboo grove tomorrow when the sun is at the highest point. Now go, all of you!"

After making sure they were not followed, the group returned to the cave. Gahdar told Sahbaar of Rahshar's threat. "I will never let him harm you!" Nero roared.

The white and brown tiger had to make a decision. Cheerah had been making trips to the place where Man was healing Bahar and Ahgrah, and she brought progress reports back often. Ahgrah was doing very well, and after some uncertainty, Bahar finally started to improve. He would live and be healthy also. However, the gibbon didn't know how much longer it would take for them to return. Sahbaar decided he couldn't wait for them any longer. He addressed his best friend.

"Nero, you are my dearest friend. I would never let anything happened to any of you to save myself. It is time for me to face Rahshar. I will go and fight for what is just, but I will not meet him in the field by the bamboo grove. That field is a small and insignificant place, like I'm sure Rahshar thinks our conflict is. Tell him I will only meet him at the Gathering Place. I want to confront him where anyone can come and see justice prevail!" Nero bounded off and delivered his friend's message.

Dawn arrived quietly. Throughout the jungle, there was a solemn peacefulness in the air. Nero had come up with a plan. The night before, he and the others had gone around to any animals they could find, telling them of the meeting between the tiger and the King. Each friend encouraged everyone to attend, and also to ask others to come. As the sun began to climb in the sky, small groups began to make their way to the Gathering Place.

The tiger crawled out of the cave and sat blinking in the bright midday sunlight. He took a deep breath, stretched out his shoulders and chest, then stood and began to walk tall and proud. As he made his way down the path, animals watched him from around trees and through bushes. After a while, a few young ones began to follow him from a short distance, defying their parent's commands not to. The crowd grew, and soon older animals began to join the procession. Of course, Sahbaar couldn't help but notice the growing crowd following him. No one seemed to be afraid of him. It was as if he was not different at all.

Soon, Sahbaar and his followers reached the Gathering Place. Sahbaar looked around slowly in awe. The hillsides were crowded with animals. The tiger had never seen so many animals together at one time, not even at the New Moon Gathering. Sahbaar was humbled that all these animals would be interested in his fate.

The tiger walked slowly to the center of the small field and sat down. The animals who had followed him quickly began to fit into the crowd along the sides of the field wherever they could. Nero had told Sahbaar's family about the meeting the night before. Sahandra was worried little Alandra would become too upset witnessing this confrontation, but the mother tiger had to be there. Lambara volunteered to stay back at the lair with his daughter. When Sahandra arrived, Nero ushered her over to a spot he had reserved for her on the edge of the field behind her son.

The crowd was very large, as nearly the whole jungle had come to see Sahbaar's fate. The animals all began to talk amongst themselves, trying to predict what would happen as they waited impatiently for the confrontation to begin. They did not have to wait long, as the King and Jungle Council soon arrived and assembled on the Council platform.

Sahbaar and Rahshar stared at each other for some time. Then the King began to pace. Stopping to face Sahbaar, he sat. "Sahbaar," he began in a booming voice, "you have broken the Jungle Council decree of banishment by returning to this jungle. As punishment, you will be led to the edge of the Black Circle, where you will cast yourself in."

"No!" screamed Sahandra, and two huge bears grabbed her as she tried to lunge at Rahshar. The whole crowd gasped at the news and began to mutter and whisper to each other. The Black Circle was a pit that was so deep that it remained dark even when the sun shined directly down onto it. It was not known how deep it was, or what lay at the bottom. No one had ever really been forced to jump in, though some threats had been made in the past. This time, however, the King seemed determined to carry out the punishment.

"This is madness!" Nero shouted, stepping forward. "Sahbaar is a hero! He saved us all from Man!" Two more bears hurried to hold him and force him back into the crowd.

"Silence!" Rahshar roared. "A decree has been violated! The Council has spoken!"

"The Council is wrong!" Gahdar shouted back. "The decree was wrong!" More bears silenced the rhino also.

Rahshar stood again and looked at Sahbaar angrily. "I must say I am concerned about your friends, Sahbaar. In the past, there have been rumors of them breaking the law by going to see you during your banishment. Even my own son has been influenced by your friendship. These have only been rumors which could not be proven, but now your friends have openly insulted and challenged the Council and myself. For this alone, they could be punished severely. This behavior also makes the rumors of the past seem more likely, which would make them as guilty as you. Should they be punished in the same way?" he asked looking around. The mothers of Sahbaar's friends began to call out, begging for mercy, but Sahbaar's voice was the loudest.

"No!" he roared, leaping to his feet. "Please, spare them. I'm sure I'm responsible for anything they might have done. They are not guilty, and should not be punished."

Rahshar looked thoughtful. "Just to show I can be merciful, I may spare them. Y*our* fate, however, is sealed!" Sahbaar stared back at the lion defiantly.

Akoorah, who had been sitting on a tree branch near the edge of the field, flew over and landed in front of the King, bowing. "I am but a visitor to your jungle, and so I do not know your ways," she began, "but elsewhere, someone in the tiger's position would be allowed to plead his case."

"Yes, yes!" the animals began to call out. "Let him plead his case." "Give him a chance to tell the story!" others said. Still others shouted, "Let the different one speak!"

Rahshar began to pace the platform's edge again. "Plead his case? Tell his story? Do you mean those rumors that everyone has been spreading throughout the jungle? Yes, I have heard them, and that is exactly what they are, just stories. Stories conjured up so that Sahbaar has a reason to come back to this jungle, and to make him a hero so that he could stay."

"You're wrong! It's all true!" Gahdar shouted before the bear could grab his horn again.

"True?!" Rahshar went on, continuing to pace. "If these stories are all true, why is it when I tried to find someone who had witnessed this last great battle, none could be found?" It was true. The few witnesses there had been were all too afraid to admit seeing anything, for fear the King would punish them for not reporting the tiger right away.

Sahbaar was discouraged. "No one else saw? How can this be?!" He looked around the crowd worriedly.

Rahshar continued attacking the white tiger with his words. "Actually, there were a few of my own guards who claimed they witnessed your last encounter with Man," he started, sounding almost sincere. Sahbaar looked up hopefully. Perhaps these guards would defend him. Rahshar sneered as he continued. "You were no great hero! In fact, what they saw was the dark Man from the other jungle capturing the strange pale Man, the enemy. You did nothing! In fact, one guard even says he saw your friend Cheerah bring some of the pale enemy Man into our jungle!"

"No, no," Sahbaar tried to explain. "Not all of the pale Man are our enemy. The ones Cheerah brought are good, and they came to help! They took the bad pale Man away!"

Rahshar suddenly stopped and stared right at the tiger. "If they are so good," he sputtered excitedly, "then why did they also take some of the animals away? Your other friends, no less!" The crowd noises grew.

"They took animals injured by the evil Man away to heal them!"

Sahbaar roared back. "Cheerah brought them to help!"

"Where is Cheerah?" Rahshar asked suddenly. "She isn't even here to defend herself. Could it be your friends are beginning to abandon you?"

"Cheerah has gone to check on the injured animals, as she has been doing for weeks now," Sahbaar said quietly but firmly. "If you ask me, she is the real hero, knowing of this Man who can help heal our fellow creatures. As for me, I never sought to be a hero. I just tried to do my part to save us all from the bad Man."

The crowd had become silent when the cats began to get loud, but now Sahbaar's last speech made them all began to murmur their approval. Even Rahshar sat a moment, looking at the tiger as he thought about Sahbaar's words. Then, he shook his head with a frown, turned, and walked back to talk with the Council.

Sahbaar sat and looked around helplessly at the crowd. His friends and family, who were still being held by the bears, looked back at him with sadness in their eyes. It certainly seemed like Rahshar was determined to win. Sahbaar couldn't think of anything else to say. He needed a way to let Rahshar see the truth; that he was no threat, and the Man Cheerah brought were good.

As if his wish had been answered, the sounds of the murmuring crowd were interrupted by a noise familiar to the white and brown tiger and his friends; the sound of a moving Man lair growling a short distance away. Just then, some monkey sentinels came scampering through the treetops to inform the King that Man had returned to the jungle. As they reported this, the sound of the lair stopped. The entire jungle crowd became silent. As Rahshar was about to tell the animals to scatter, the noise started up again but this time faded away.

Then Cheerah made her way through a bush. "Why is everyone gathered here?" she asked a water buffalo.

As the water buffalo told the gibbon of the meeting, there was another noise in the bushes, and Ahgrah crawled through. "Sahbaar!" the crocodile called, not realizing what was going on. "Are you all right? I thought the Man's stick might have gotten you!" Ignoring the crowd, she crawled quickly out to her friend. Animals all around the field, especially crocodiles, gasped when they saw her scars. Sahbaar was equally shocked.

"Ahgrah, are you truly all right?" he asked, his eyes wide with wonder.

Ahgrah was very cheerful. "Yes, I am fine now. I was very sick for a long time, but the Man Cheerah knows made me all well again." She looked cross - eyed at the scars on her snout, then over her shoulder at the ones on her back and tail. "All except for those marks. Cheerah and I think I will always have those now, but I don't mind at all. They make me different from all other crocodiles, unique, like you, Sahbaar!" she said with a huge grin.

"Did you hear that?" Sahbaar called to Rahshar. "Another different one! Are you going to banish her, too?" The crowd laughed softly.

Cheerah scampered out to Sahbaar. "I just heard what has been going on. I guess we all got back just in time!"

"We all?" Sahbaar looked at Cheerah and Ahgrah and then began to scan the crowd quickly. "Where is Bahar? He is all right, isn't he? Oh, tell me he's all right!" the tiger began to plead.

Cheerah grabbed the tiger's shoulder to steady him. "Calm down, Sahbaar. Bahar is all right." Then the gibbon began to giggle and twitch. "Oh, he is much better than all right!"

"So, where is he?" Sahbaar said firmly, scanning the crowd again. "I don't see him."

Cheerah rolled her eyes. "Oh, he is probably out somewhere practicing."

Now Sahbaar was totally confused. "Practicing? Practicing what?" Cheerah had been holding her breath, waiting for the tiger to say those very words. When he did, she exploded into wild laughter, and began running around in circles, doing backflips and cartwheels. Ahgrah also began to laugh as if she too knew the joke. Everyone looked at the pair as if they were crazy.

Rahshar was not amused. "Silence, you two! This is a serious matter!" he roared, "especially for you, gibbon!" Cheerah ignored the threat and began a happy dance.

Just then, Bahar's head poked through a bush. "Cheerah, are you here?" he asked. Seeing the crowd, and his nephew sitting in the middle of the field, he added, "What is going on?" Once Sahandra saw him, she gasped. The tiger tried to break the bear's hold so that she could run to him.

"Wait!" Cheerah suddenly shouted, leaping in front of the female tiger and putting up a hairy paw to stop her. The gibbon looked back at Bahar and thrust out her other flat palm. "You wait too, please." Then, she turned to face Rahshar, and her face became tense and serious as she began to speak in a loud, firm voice. "I have been told what you have said about the friendships I have with the Man outside our jungle. You say this is bad, and they are evil. You say all these creatures are the same, and they only wish to harm us. Well, see what they have done for Bahar!" With that, she waved to the tiger, which leaped out of the bushes with great force.

Those who remembered Bahar as a young lame tiger were so stunned they fell backward as the creature that once even had a hard time walking began to run around the field at a dizzying speed. Bahar happily and proudly raced around the edge of the field four times. He then ran to the center of the field and held his bad leg up for all to see. It had an artificial extension attached to it. "Cheerah's Man has made me a leg! Now, at last, I can run and hunt as a tiger is meant to!" he shouted. The crowd cheered as Sahandra ran over to him.

Rahshar didn't know what to say. As the tiger continued to hold up the leg extension made by the doctors, animals from all sides of the field ran out to see the wondrous thing. The King began to pace again, trying to think. "Silence, all of you!" he roared finally. "Back to your places!" The animals all meekly returned to the edges of the field. Only Sahandra stayed to be with her brother, who she thought she had lost again forever.

It took a while for the murmurs of the crowd to die down. Rahshar cleared his throat and began again. "It is true that what Cheerah's Man has done for you is a great thing. They are truly clever. However, what we are meeting about here today is the breaking of a decree and the punishment for that."

"The breaking of a *foolish* decree," Sahbaar corrected him. "Say, now that Bahar has four good legs, he is no longer different, so he no longer needs to be banished. *I* should go see Cheerah's Man. Perhaps they can make me orange!" The crowd burst into laughter and began cheering again.

"For the last time, this is not about Man!" Rahshar roared over the crowd.

"Man is a part of this," Cheerah suddenly spoke up. "It is about them as well as us. It is about those who are different. Let me show you something, please!" She turned and scampered off into the bushes. The crowd began to murmur again, and Rahshar started to pace. Soon, the gibbon reappeared dragging something large and flat. The animals had never seen anything like it. It had many layers of brown flat leaves, but it was no plant. "I took this from Man," Cheerah began, holding up the book. "The female Man-cub likes to show it to me when I am there. It has many markings of things in the jungle." The gibbon flipped the pages to show the pictures to the King.

"Why did you bring this thing?" Rahshar asked impatiently. "How can it help us?"

"It shows many things," the gibbon continued. "I just never understood it before."

"Get to the point!" the King growled. Cheerah began to turn to certain pages she had marked. "This shows that there are several kinds of Man. See, the pale ones, the dark ones, the dark ones who are also partly white ..."

"Yes, we know about that!" Rahshar interrupted. "We agree there are many kinds of Man!"

"But here," Cheerah pointed. "The dark Man with the stripes are with a tiger like Sahbaar. In fact, I believe they paint the white on themselves to create brown stripes."

"Yes!" Sahbaar added excitedly, "I have seen them do so!"

"So?" Rahshar snapped. "What does all this mean?"

"I believe these Man think a tiger like Sahbaar is very special, certainly not an outcast." The gibbon turned to Sahbaar. "How did these creatures behave towards you?" she asked.

Sahbaar didn't even have to think. "They hunted food for me," he began, "and always protected me from the others. That's how I used them to rescue us all from the bad pale Man."

"You see," Cheerah explained. "These Man think Sahbaar's difference is so special, they want to protect him and are even willing to change themselves to try and look like him!"

"But they are Man," Rahshar argued. "What does that matter to us?"

"Man can do many wondrous things," Cheerah continued. "You have seen Bahar's leg. If they think a difference is special, perhaps we should also. The dark Man who give themselves stripes are not the only ones who think a tiger like Sahbaar is special. See?" The gibbon held up the book and turned to several pages that had more pictures of a white tiger with brown stripes. Cheerah turned slowly as she flipped through the pictures so that all could see. "The Man-cub likes to look at these markings often. I don't think they would have been marked in this thing if they were not special. I also discovered Sahbaar is not the only special one." She pointed to two facing pages. "See the two rhinos? One has one horn, and the other has two. Every rhino I have ever seen in our jungle, including Gahdar and his family, only have one horn, but there are rhinos somewhere that have two!"

"What? I'm special?" Gahdar said with surprise and lowered his head modestly.

"Oh, no," Sahbaar remarked, pretending to be frightened. "Gahdar and his whole family are different! They must be banished!" The crowd exploded with laughter.

"Silence!" Rahshar roared again. "You are going to place the opinion of Man over that of the Council? What do you really know of these pale Man?" The animals all shook their heads and waited for the King to continue. "I have seen the pale Man before, when I was young," Rahshar said, pacing again. "There were many of them, with many of their terrible sticks. They came to hunt us, but not for food, just like the bad pale Man who were just here. We learned to fear them. How are we to know that Cheerah's Man are not really just like them?" The Council, the bear guards, and some others agreed with the King, and growled their approval.

Cheerah raised her arms to get everyone's attention. "You say these Man came to the jungle long ago," she nearly shouted at Rahshar, "but there have been none since then until these last three. It has been so long that most of us did not even know of them. When the Man who are my friends saw the bad ones, they took them away, and all their sticks, too. I can now remember them taking sticks away from other Man at their lair. I tell you, they are good, and I think they may even protect us! It may very well be the Man who I know who keep more bad Man from coming to our jungle!"

"Good Man, bad Man, these are all just stories you are telling me. Without proof, what can I say?" the King replied casually.

"Wha - wha -" Sahbaar sputtered. "You said yourself that your own guards saw what happened. Surely they would know if Cheerah speaks the truth!"

The bear guards, who had not really been paying attention, now became very nervous. They had not told the King that part of the story for fear it would anger him and get them in trouble somehow. "Tell the truth," the King growled. "Is their story true? Did Cheerah's pale Man take the evil pale Man away?" After squirming and fidgeting and looking around for a few minutes, the bear guards all reluctantly agreed with Cheerah's story. The crowd began to murmur again, and the King was genuinely surprised.

"So, some Man are good," Rahshar finally admitted, "but that does not change things! The real fact is, Sahbaar brought these bad Man to our jungle, and that became a threat to us all. I told you something like this would happen. That is why I had him banished. If I was to spare him from the Black Circle this time, there is no way we could keep him banished. He has shown us that. Each time he came back to this jungle could pose a new threat to us all. Therefore, I have no choice but to carry out the Black Circle punishment! This matter is now closed. The Council has spoken, and the accused will be led to his fate." The females in the crowd all cried out in horror, and Sahandra fainted.

Four bears stepped forward to take their places, two on either side of the disappointed tiger. Other bears ushered Sahbaar's family and friends back to the edge of the field, and one gently picked up Sahandra and laid her next to Bahar. Like the rest of Sahbaar's friends, Akoorah was stunned. She couldn't believe there was nothing more that could be done. The bird decided to try one more thing.

"Excuse me" she addressed the King. "Where I come from, it is customary to let the condemned say one last thing. Would that be permitted here?"

Rahshar looked around at the solemn crowd. "I suppose that would be all right," he growled softly. "Sahbaar, what last thing do you have to say?"

Sahbaar turned to face the crowd. Looking around humbly, he began in a soft voice. "Creatures of the jungle, I'm sorry for any problems I may have created. I do feel I have done more good than harm. I also feel this decision is wrong, but because it was decided by the Jungle Council, I will abide by it." Sahandra, who had just woken up, began to sob when she heard these words. Sahbaar took a deep breath and began to speak louder. "King Rahshar says that what this is all about is the fact that I defied my banishment. *I* believe this is about the cause of my banishment, the fact that I am different." The tiger paused and began to pace in a circle as he thought.

He faced the crowd once more. "Today, we have heard many things about Man. Though the King feels they have no importance, I think we can learn some things from them. As we have discovered, there are different kinds of Man, some with dark hides, and some with pale. We have also learned that different Man act differently. The dark Man who paint white on themselves care for me, the ones who don't have stripes would rather hunt me. However, it has also been discovered the Man who look very much alike, like the pale ones, can act very differently. Some treat us well, some do not. They are the same, yet we do not know right away which is our friend."

"What does all this matter?" Rahshar growled. "You should be saying goodbye to your family!"

Akoorah flapped her wings in the King's face. "It is very undignified to interrupt someone's last words," she scolded. "Hush!" The King actually looked embarrassed.

"We have seen the differences in Man," Sahbaar continued more confidently, "but now we find a strange similarity. The dark Man who make themselves look like me, are good to me and anyone I am with, and so are the pale Man Cheerah knows. How can this be? How can two groups of the same kind of creature, who are obviously so different, behave the same?" This made the whole crowd think, including the Council and Rahshar himself. After leaving them all struggling to find an answer, Sahbaar suggested one. "Could it be," he said in his most convincing tone, "that just because someone is different doesn't automatically make them a threat? Someone may be different because that's just the way they were born. That's no reason to make them an outcast." With that, the tiger lowered his head and turned away, ready to be led off.

Some of the females in the crowd could be heard sobbing softly, and everyone felt very uncomfortable. The King seemed almost concerned for a moment, but he quickly got up to lead the Council and Sahbaar to the Black Circle. When he turned, he was surprised to see the Council had stepped back and gathered in a tight group without him. Before he could approach them, they finished their meeting and stepped to the front of the platform.

Maharah the old elephant moved to the center. "The Council has listened to the accused, and what he says makes sense." Rahshar's jaw dropped in surprise. Maharah continued. "We in the Council are thought of as the wisest animals in the jungle, but we readily admit we can still learn from the young." He smiled at Sahbaar. "We now believe this white and brown tiger poses no threat to the jungle, whether he be different or not, and so the punishment for breaking his banishment, and the banishment itself, are hereby canceled."

A huge cheer went up throughout the crowd. Rahshar was furious. "The Council had already decided on the punishment!" he roared, silencing the animals. "You can't change your vote simply because the accused has tried to make you feel guilty!"

"The Council, the Council!" Maharah snapped, turning to face Rahshar. "For the longest time, 'the Council' has been nothing more than a group of timid animals letting you have your way because we were all frightened of you! Thanks to this brave tiger, we have come to realize we were not living up to our duty to serve this jungle honestly. That stops today!" The elephant turned back towards the crowd. "As I was saying, Sahbaar's punishment and banishment are hereby canceled, and the same goes for Bahar." Maharah looked down at the stunned tiger and his equally stunned uncle. "Go ahead, Sahbaar. Go be with your family."

There were tears of joy in Sahbaar's eyes as he turned carefully, as if afraid someone might change the ruling again. When he saw his family waiting for him, he bounded over as the crowd exploded with cheers once again. Rahshar turned and dropped his head in shame and embarrassment. A few of the Council members called to him, but he did not stop. Instead, he trudged off into the jungle by himself.

From that time on, there was a great sense of joy in the jungle. Sahbaar was busy all the time, spending equal amounts of time with his family and his friends. He loved to play with his sister, though he knew there would come a time when he would be ready to find a mate and start his own family. When that time came, he decided he would make his own home in the rock tower cave in the other jungle, where he had grown up.

Sahbaar took all his family and friends to see the Koo Doo native tribe. Sahbaar's friends looked on from the bushes so as not to frighten the strange Man as they scurried about bringing food to the white and brown tiger and his amazed family. The natives were not the only ones still interested in this rare tiger. When Cheerah took the book back to the Man camp, one of her Man friends caught her. Instead of punishing her, he turned to the pictures of the white and brown tiger and pointed at them excitedly. Cheerah knew he was the doctor who had seen Sahbaar, and wanted to see him again. As she had done before, she led this Man group back into the jungle, and then went off to find her friend.

When Sahbaar appeared, all the men gasped and pulled out strange looking rocks. When the tiger turned to flee, Cheerah recognized the cameras and told Sahbaar not to worry, they were not dangerous. It seemed as if these Man just couldn't get enough pictures. Soon after that, small Man lairs were seen running along the edges of the jungle. The Man in them rarely stopped, and when they did, it was only to look at the animals or search for something. Though there was no way for the animals to know these were game wardens who were patrolling what was now an animal preserve, the animals still somehow felt safe by having these Man around.

All this time, Rahshar was miserable. At first, the rumors were that he was deeply angered by the Council deciding against his wishes. It was only when he called a meeting at the Gathering Place that everyone learned the truth. The animals arrived to find the King already there, but not on the Council platform. Instead, he sat in the middle of the field, his head hanging, looking very humble. When the animals had finally gathered, he raised his head, which silenced the crowd.

"Dear subjects," he began in a loud, yet solemn voice. "I wish to apologize for my behavior in the Sahbaar banishment matter. Further, I would like to apologize for the way I have persecuted animals who were different before or since then." He stared at the ground again, struggling to find the words, then raised his head and continued. "When I was still a young lion, I was chosen to be the King. I was very nervous and worried that I would not do my job well. That is the reason that I formed the Jungle Council. I wanted a group of the wisest creatures who could help me make decisions, and by choosing a variety of animals for the Council, I felt I could get a good variety of opinions.

"Unfortunately, as the years went by, I let the importance of my office interfere with the decision making. In an effort to do my job the best I could and protect everyone, I became too suspicious. I tried to solve problems that weren't even there; problems I created myself. For this I am truly sorry. It took Sahbaar and Maharah's words to finally make me realize what I was doing. If you forgive me and give me another chance, I promise to try and listen to my advisors and think before I act." The lion lowered his head again.

There was a strange silence, as no one knew what to do or say. Finally, Sahbaar walked slowly into the center of the field and stood facing Rahshar. The lion was not surprised, and did not raise his head. He was certain the tiger would use this opportunity to seek some revenge. Perhaps he would even go so far as to suggest the King himself be cast into the Black Circle. It did not matter. Rahshar was so ashamed that if it was what the subjects wished, he would obey. Instead, the white and brown tiger's words were comforting and supportive.

"I will admit, there was a time when I was very angry with you because I felt you were wrong. Then, I had a long talk with my mother and father, and they told me what a good and powerful leader you were before I was born. Now that you have spoken, I can see where things went wrong, and I am no longer angry. I'm hoping the rest of the jungle will agree with me when I ask you to please continue to be our King!" After these last words,

Sahbaar looked around, and the crowd began to cheer wildly.

    Rahshar raised his head, his face a mixture of surprise and gratitude. Nero ran up to be with his father. Then, two bear guards stepped forward to raise Rahshar onto their shoulders, and two more picked up Sahbaar as well. As the bears carried the two cats around the field, the cheers went on and on... and so did a happy life for all in the jungle!

THE END

Made in the USA
Lexington, KY
17 February 2018